LEADERSHIP LESSONS
FROM THE TRENCHES

A FOLLOWER'S PERSPECTI VE

DR. MARLENA HUDSON
DEDICATION

Leadership Lessons from the Trenches was truly inspired by God. With over 20 years of experience in Human Resources, I have devoted my career to helping others grow, develop, and succeed, particularly leaders. Along the way, I have gathered numerous leadership lessons and felt compelled to share them with aspiring leaders or those seeking to enhance their leadership skills. This vision gave birth to *Leadership Lessons from the Trenches: A Follower's Perspective*.

I want to express my deepest gratitude to my wonderful husband, Howard Sr., and my amazing children, Howard Jr. and Paris. Without your love and support, this book would not have been possible. Howard Sr., the leadership insights I have learned from you are woven throughout the pages of this book. Howard Jr. and Paris, thank you for your grace and the space you allowed me to think and write. I love you with all my heart.

I also want to thank several individuals who have played a significant role in my journey. Sargent Smith, Jan Bullard, Amy Scott, Doug Keller, Scott Fredey, Dr. Steven Dykeman, Dr. Debbie Augustin, Dr. John Betterson, and Dr. Kathleen Patterson, you saw something in me and pushed me to keep going. Your prayers, encouragement, belief, and the stretch assignments you trusted me with have shaped me, and for that, I am forever grateful.

I am deeply grateful to my Talent Services team—Ana, Christina, Emily, Jasmine, Kathy, Krasynthia, Nola, Patti, and Rachael—for shaping me both as a person and as a leader!

i

A heartfelt thank you to everyone who shared their leadership insights, experiences, and stories with me. Your contributions have truly brought this book to life.

Contents

INTRODUCTION

Followership is a discipline of supporting leaders and helping them to lead well. It is not submission but the wise and good care of leaders, done out of a sense of gratitude for their willingness to take on the responsibilities of leadership and a sense of hope and faith in their abilities and potential.

~ Reverend Paul Beedle

When discussing leadership, people often speak of it as if it were a supernatural ability to achieve something extraordinary within the organizations where they hold a leadership role. However, I argue that leaders are only as effective as the followers they guide. More importantly, leaders are followers, too! Although leadership and followership may seem antithetical, they are more closely connected than many realize. To be an effective leader, one must first learn to follow. All leaders, regardless of their position, are accountable to someone or a group that monitors their progress and effectiveness. For example, frontline supervisors report to middle managers, who in turn report to executives, who are often accountable to a board of directors or investors. Every organization has its unique structure, but the core idea remains: all leaders are also followers, highlighting the intersection between these roles. If all leaders are followers, it is crucial to pay attention to their employees, the lessons they can offer, and their own experience following others.

The interconnectedness of the leader-follower relationship challenges the traditional view of leadership. In the 19th and 20th centuries, leadership was seen as a hierarchical role, where the leader held a title or position of authority and led a group of individuals who were expected to follow orders without question. Followers were often perceived as obedient subordinates who waited for instructions and kept their opinions to themselves. However, in the 21st century, relying solely on positional power is likely to lead to resentment and resistance among followers. Ira Chaleff, author and leader of the Intelligent Disobedience Movement, argues that modern followers have evolved; they now possess the courage to take responsibility, challenge the status quo and their leaders, and actively participate in organizational transformation. The era of silent, obedient followers is over. Today, followers are vocal and expect more from the leaders they choose. Yes, followers choose the leader— not the other way around. A recent DDI study found that 57% of people have quit because of their supervisor, and 37% have considered leaving because of their manager.

Being appointed to a leadership position does not automatically make someone a leader. True leadership requires at least one follower or a group of followers who support and recognize that person as a leader. What matters most is being acknowledged as a leader by others.

Leadership experts James Kouzes and Barry Posner have noted that "leadership is in the eye of the beholder." Reverend Paul Beedle also emphasized that followers place their hope and faith in a leader's abilities and potential, making it better to have willing followers than a group that despises their leadership. In today's world, leaders who rely solely on positional power are likely to face resistance. There is a crucial difference between exerting authority and influencing others. Influence garners more commitment and buy-in from followers to achieve organizational goals. While positional power may be necessary in certain situations, effective leaders must know when to use both positional and personal power.

The title of this book, *Leadership Lessons from the Trenches: A Follower's Perspective of Leadership*, reflects the idea that nothing compares to the insights and knowledge gained through hands-on, realworld experience in challenging situations. The phrase "from the trenches" is a metaphor borrowed from military terminology, where soldiers in trenches face direct combat and navigate difficult and unpredictable circumstances.

Leaders who have been deeply involved in day-to-day operations, facing and overcoming obstacles alongside their teams, are often better equipped to lead. They have hands-on experience and understand what it takes to motivate and guide a group based on personal experiences. Their leadership style tends to be practical, hard-earned, and grounded in reality rather than theoretical or abstract. Leading from the trenches emphasizes that true leadership skills are developed not just through formal education or high-level strategy but through the experiences of working through tough challenges, making difficult decisions, and navigating complex real-world dynamics.

From an employee's perspective, leadership is often defined by the actions, attitudes, and behaviors of those in leadership roles. Employees observe and interpret these elements, forming key leadership lessons that can shape their own approach to leadership. By being attentive to their employees' experiences, leaders can learn important lessons that enhance their leadership effectiveness and contribute to a healthier, more productive workplace culture.

For the past 20 years, I have worked as an Organizational Development practitioner and led talent development teams within Human Resources across various organizations. During this time, I have gathered valuable leadership lessons through my own experiences and from guiding and advising leaders. I have witnessed both the positive and negative aspects of leadership and will share practical lessons from a follower's perspective. Additionally, I have had the privilege of engaging with colleagues from diverse backgrounds who have shared their stories and insights on effective leadership.

Here are some of the questions I explored with this group:

1. What behaviors do non-leaders expect from their leaders?

2. Can you share an example of a leader who has positively impacted your career?

3. What are some of the biggest frustrations you've encountered with your supervisor?

4. Do you have any stories or examples that illustrate your concerns with leadership?

5. If you could offer advice to your supervisor on how they could improve as a leader, what would you suggest?

Based on these discussions, I have compiled the following leadership lessons:

1. Effective Leadership

2. The Humble Leader: Tame Your Ego

3. Mastering the Art of Connection

4. Uncharted Territory

5. Essential Communication: The Key to Success and Collaboration

6. Distributed Power

7. Decrease Subjectivity and Increase Objectivity

8. Honest and Sincere Appreciation

9. The Career Architect

Each chapter of this book outlines valuable lessons that leaders can learn throughout their journey, emphasizing the importance of focusing on their employees as well as drawing on their own practical experiences as followers. At the end of each chapter, I invite readers to reflect on their leadership journey and consider how they might alter or enhance their behavior to become even more effective leaders.

CHAPTER 1

Effective Leadership

Leadership is not about a title or designation. It's about impact, influence, and inspiration. Impact involves getting results, influence is about spreading the passion you have for your work, and you have to inspire teammates and customers.

~ Robin Sharma, author

Choosing to step into a leadership role can be a challenging decision for many. Some may question their preparedness, while others feel confident and ready to lead from the outset. Those stepping into leadership roles, whether as a first-time supervisor or an executive, often face high expectations. With these expectations comes the pressure to succeed and demonstrate capability in the new position.

Marshall Goldsmith, author of *What Got You Here Won't Get You There*, highlights that many technical leaders are selected based on their intelligence, expertise, and ability to deliver results independently (Goldsmith, 2010). However, leadership demands a different skill set. Due to their previous achievements, individuals may have a preconceived notion of what it takes to transition from an individual contributor to a leadership role, which can sometimes lead to an overestimation of their readiness.

In leadership, success is no longer measured by personal achievements but by the ability to inspire and guide others toward a shared vision, goal, or task. As Jack Welch, former CEO of General Electric, wisely stated, "Before you are a leader, success is all about growing yourself. When you become a leader, success is all about growing others" (Welch, n.d.).

Understanding your purpose, values, and goals is an exciting initial step. Begin by shaping your personal leadership narrative and vision to become the best leader you can be.

This chapter will delve into the essence of leadership, the different styles, and the important role followers play. Additionally, you'll have the chance to reflect on your purpose, values, and personal goals as you develop your leadership identity.

Effective Leadership

The success of leaders is vital to an organization's success regardless of the industry. They craft a vision for the future, guide the way toward achieving it, inspire their teams to meet their goals, and foster a positive work environment. Effective leadership has a profound impact on employee engagement, job satisfaction, productivity, and the overall performance of the organization.

But what defines effective leadership? For decades, researchers have examined various behaviors, traits, and qualities of successful leaders, but a universally accepted definition remains elusive. Leadership is shaped by specific contexts and is the result of complex interactions between leaders, followers, and the environment. Factors such as technological innovation, globalization, and economic conditions have influenced evolving views on what it takes to be an effective leader. After reviewing many definitions of leadership, I developed this description: "A leader or group of leaders who foster a high level of motivation and commitment among followers to collaboratively achieve future-oriented goals."

Additionally, leaders possess certain traits that either draw followers in or push them away. Ralph Stogdill, a leading scholar in leadership studies and former Professor Emeritus at Ohio State University, conducted extensive research on leadership traits between 1904 and 1948. He identified traits such as intelligence, alertness, insight, responsibility, initiative, persistence, self confidence, and sociability as critical for leadership. In a subsequent study in 1974, Stogdill refined his findings to highlight the importance of drive, persistence, risk-taking, self-confidence, decision-making, stress management, emotional maturity, influence, and sociability (Northouse, 2022).

To be an effective leader, individuals must:

- Have one or more willing followers and be able to follow others.

- Exhibit characteristics of a leader to motivate followers and garner commitment.

- Be inspirational and unite the team towards a common goal.

- Lead followers towards something greater than themselves–a vision for the future. The idea must be clear and vivid, and they must be able to effectively communicate it so followers know what needs to be done to make it a reality.

- Create an environment where all followers feel respected and cared for, and encourage the team to build mutually respectful relationships. Followers must be able to work together to achieve futuristic goals.

- Recognize team member's gifts and talents to position them for success. Investing in another person's success garners a high level of motivation.

Effective leaders must possess several characteristics and skills to inspire commitment from their followers, including integrity, competence, humility, accountability, excellent communication, decisiveness, empathy, and good listening. However, personal characteristics alone are insufficient. Leaders must have the skills and capabilities to manage systems and processes and lead people simultaneously.

The Difference and Connection Between Leadership and Management

In a Harvard Business Review article, Abraham Zaleznik pointed out that the distinction between managers and leaders lies in their mindset. Managers prioritize processes, seek stability, and make swift decisions (Zaleznik, 2004). In contrast, leaders excel in uncertainty, embrace a lack of structure, and delay decisions until they have a full grasp of the situation (Zaleznik, 2004).

Warren Bennis (2009), in his book *On Becoming a Leader*, further highlighted the differences between the two:

Managers	Leaders

• Administers	• Innovates
• Monitor Others	• Develops Others
• Focuses on systems and structures	• Focuses on people
• Maintain control	• Inspires trust
• Short-term strategic thinking	• Long-term strategic thinking
• Accepts the status quo	• Challenges the status quo
• Do things right	• Does the right thing
• Focus on the bottom line and getting results	• Maintains a strategic foresight

Leadership scholars have devoted substantial effort to distinguishing between management and leadership. However, I contend that both are essential for effective leadership. Expecting one individual to excel in every leadership trait is unrealistic—to do so would be God-like, perfect in a sense. Instead, leaders identify areas for growth and either:

1. Create a plan for personal development in those areas, or

2. Build a team of people who possess those strengths and rely on them to bridge the gaps.

Leaders must stay focused on achieving goals (managing) while recognizing that the world is always evolving, requiring constant strategic thinking and foresight (leadership).

Full Range Leadership Development

John Sosik and Dongil Jung (2011) developed the Full Range Leadership Development (FRLD) model, which accounts for varying leadership styles, ranging from avoidant to transformational and everything in between. There are four major leadership styles:

Avoidant	**Corrective**	**Transactional**	**Transformational**
Laissez Faire	Active	Contingent	4Is of
Passive	Managementby-	Reward	Transformation
Managementby-	Exception		
Exception			

Avoidant Leaders

An avoidant leader is often described as embodying laissez-faire and passive management-by-exception styles. Such leaders lack a sense of responsibility for their own development or that of their team. They fail to respond to urgent requests, avoid decision-making, and delegate the responsibility for achieving goals to their team members. Essentially, they hold the title of leader but are only there for the paycheck, making this the least effective form of leadership. Avoidant leaders tend to disengage and have minimal interaction with their staff. When employees bring up questions or concerns to such a supervisor, they are unlikely to receive a response, leaving them to resolve issues on their own. This leadership style is characterized by staying isolated in their office and rarely communicating with or engaging their team.

Similarly, passive managers who lead by exception are equally ineffective. They are reactive rather than proactive, intervening only when problems arise. Passive leaders allow their teams to operate independently, which can result in team members lacking a clear vision and direction. The lack of active leadership affects the team's overall performance, resulting in low morale and misalignment of organizational goals and objectives. In both instances, their team members have low trust, respect, and confidence in them as leaders.

Corrective Leaders

Corrective leaders, who actively manage by exception, are marginally more effective than avoidant leaders but still fall short. Their team often perceives them as micromanagers, as they prefer to take charge of resolving issues themselves rather than coaching their team through corrective actions. These leaders are seen as average performers who function best in hierarchical environments. In such settings, employees fear making mistakes and operate under a "failure is not an option" mentality. This fear discourages them from speaking up or sharing dissenting opinions, leading to organizational silence, which hampers creativity and innovation. Consequently, the organization remains stagnant and does not flourish under these leaders.

Transactional Leadership

James MacGregor Burns perceives transactional leadership as a formal agreement between leaders and employees, where leaders emphasize achieving results and assess success based on an organization's reward and penalty system (Burns, 2004). FRLD refers to this type of leadership as contingent reward (Sosik & Jung, 2011). For instance, contingent reward leaders set objectives and clarify expectations for their employees. Employees are then responsible for meeting these goals. If they succeed, they receive rewards; if they fail, they face consequences, such as performance improvement plans or termination.

Contrary to common belief, transactional leadership can be effective in various contexts, such as sales teams, sports, or emergencies. In sales, teams operate on a contractual basis: leaders set targets, and employees strive to meet or exceed them, with rewards for success and repercussions for failure. Similarly, sports teams are rewarded based on their performance—winning competitions can lead to higher paychecks and endorsements. In emergencies, the reward often comes from successfully solving problems and the personal satisfaction of saving lives and property.

For a contractual relationship to be successful, it must benefit both parties. The organization meets its goals, and employees are rewarded for their contributions. If the relationship ceases to be beneficial, either party can end the contract.

Transformational Leadership

The transformational leadership model was initially created by sociologist James V. Downtown and further refined by James MacGregor Burns in the 1970s. This model consists of four key elements: idealized influence, inspirational motivation, intellectual stimulation, and individualized consideration (Northouse, 2022). For a leader to be deemed transformational, all these components must be present in their leadership style.

1. Idealized Influence

Idealized influence focuses on the emotional aspects of leadership. Leaders who demonstrate idealized influence embody high moral standards, virtues, character strengths, and a strong work ethic. Essentially, such leaders set high standards and earn the respect of their followers and others.

2. Inspirational Motivation

Inspirational motivation fosters emotional bonds, trust, and a sense of commitment with their followers. Transformational leaders present their followers with a compelling vision and a sense of mission, guiding them toward a common goal. This vision unites followers and equips them with the necessary knowledge and skills to achieve the desired outcomes, thereby enhancing the organization's overall performance.

3. Intellectual Stimulation

Intellectual stimulation addresses followers' needs while encouraging them to use creative problem-solving techniques. Diverse perspectives and opinions are essential to engage employees. This often prompts employees to question the underlying assumptions within the organization and challenge the status quo. It also promotes unconventional thinking to solve complex problems. The leader's responsibility is to foster an environment where employees feel psychologically safe to question organizational norms and be creative and innovative with their ideas.

4. Individualized Consideration

Leaders who recognize and appreciate each employee's unique talents, skills, and abilities exhibit individualized consideration. They take the time to understand their employees on a personal level, showing empathy and compassion while coaching them toward excellence. These leaders are aware of their employees' strengths and areas for growth, and they consistently challenge them to develop further.

The Full Range Leadership Development model accounts for varying leadership styles. Avoidant and corrective leadership styles are ineffective. These types of leaders do not promote loyalty among employees. The opposite happens—employees do not trust or respect them. Transactional leaders only work in certain environments with a cost-benefit relationship, and employees are motivated by something else (e.g., money) rather than the leader. Conversely, transformational leadership is the highest form of leadership, garnering admiration and respect from their employees.

Which style is most effective?

Some scholars assert that effective leadership requires a blend of transactional and transformational styles, as different situations demand different approaches. Transactional leadership is essential for achieving short-term goals, while transformational leadership is necessary for longterm vision and change. Style theory suggests that leaders who do not possess both styles are less effective.

The Latin prefix "Trans" means across, beyond, or through. The term "Action" implies getting things done, so transactional leadership means accomplishing tasks through others. This style focuses more on the task or goal than on the individuals performing it. Transactional leadership has advantages, such as providing clear structure, achievable goals, and straightforward motivation. However, it also has drawbacks, including inflexibility and rigidity, which can limit collaboration and innovation. For example, Vince Lombardi, the renowned American Football Coach, prioritized winning the Super Bowl above all else. His leadership philosophy, shaped by his time at West Point, was centered on execution and command and control. Lombardi's perfectionism and authoritative nature demanded excellence both on and off the field. He was known for his strict and demanding demeanor, often yelling and reprimanding those who underperformed and expecting absolute respect from everyone around him. In a book on the Green Bay Packers by Don Guilbrandsen, there is a quote that stood out from Gary Knafelc, a player for the Green Bay Packers, once said, "I feared Lombardi more than any defensive end or linebacker I ever played against. I only had to deal with those guys once or twice a year. I saw Lombardi every day" (Guilbrandsen, 2011). Lombardi's leadership led to several Super Bowl victories, a measure of success, but his harsh methods left a lasting impact on those he led. He showed little empathy for his team, adhering to a model of "do your job or get out of the way."

On the contrary, formation refers to the action of forming or the process of being formed. Transformational leaders fundamentally alter an organization or market, making it unrecognizable from its previous state. These leaders focus less on meeting immediate performance goals and more on understanding and leveraging the underlying motivations of

16

their employees to inspire them to achieve visionary, long-term organizational objectives.

Consider Jeff Bezos, founder and CEO of Amazon. When he founded Amazon in 1994, online shopping was not widespread. Initially, Amazon struggled with poor earnings because consumers were accustomed to brick-and-mortar stores. Fung Global Retail & Technology noted that as technology advanced, so did the appeal of online shopping, with its convenience, wider selections, and lower prices. This shift led to the closure of more than 5,300 stores in 2017, a 218% increase over 2016.

Mr. Bezos is a visionary leader who never wavered from his aspirational goal to transform retail shopping and grow the e-commerce industry, resulting in what is now known as the Amazon Effect. This phenomenon disrupted traditional retail and bolstered the rise of e-commerce, significantly altering the retail landscape.

Both transactional and transformational leadership styles are effective in different organizational contexts. The most successful leaders integrate elements of both, utilizing the upper levels of the Full Range Leadership Development model. Solely transactional leaders may leave their teams feeling unfulfilled in their work relationships, while exclusively transformational leaders might seem disconnected and out of touch with the day-to-day realities of their employees.

To achieve a balanced approach, leaders need to be visionary and set a clear direction for aspirational goals. They should provide timely and constructive feedback that motivates employees and fosters an innovative and inclusive environment. This environment should empower employees and provide the necessary resources for success. Leaders must be adaptable, using either a directive or inspirational approach based on the situation and the abilities of their employees.

Additionally, leaders must inspire accountability and hold employees responsible for achieving desired results. They must lead by example, consistently demonstrating the values and behaviors they expect from their team.

By adopting these practices, leaders can effectively blend transactional and transformational leadership styles, achieving both immediate and long-term success while maintaining a motivated and engaged team.

A Note on Followership

Ira Chaleff, author of *The Courageous Follower*, observed that many people instinctively react negatively to the term "followership," associating it with an outdated notion of followers as passive subordinates who merely awaited instructions and refrained from sharing their opinions (Chaleff, 2010). However, the concept of followership has evolved—followers are now seen as active partners in the leadership process. It is a collaborative dynamic in which followers willingly accept guidance and direction while also respectfully speaking up when they disagree. Leadership expert Peter Northouse defines followership as individuals who accept the influence of others to work toward a shared goal (Northouse, 2022).

While leadership often garners the spotlight, it is the followers who truly elevate someone into a leader, shifting the focus from individual contributions to collective, team-oriented success. Some may assume they are leaders based on their title, position, or status within a group. However, without a mutual and constructive relationship between leaders and followers, the essence of leadership becomes hollow and ineffective.

For true leadership to exist, there must be at least one willing follower. The emphasis here is on the word *willing*, which the Oxford Dictionary defines as ready, eager, or prepared to act. Leaders who rely on control or coercion may secure compliance from their followers, but they fail to earn respect and are often regarded as poor or ineffective bosses.

Derek Sivers, in his *First Follower: Leadership Lessons from Dancing Guy*, highlighted the pivotal role of the first follower, who transforms an individual into a leader and initiates the transition from individual accomplishments to collective efforts toward a common goal (Sivers, 2010). Chaleff (2010) also emphasized that both leaders and followers revolve around a shared purpose, not around the leaders themselves. Followers contribute to helping leaders achieve organizational goals, but they do so as engaged participants rather than blindly or passively following the leader's direction.

Lessons from the Trenches

A colleague who works in Human Resources for a major aerospace company recently shared a leadership challenge they face. The organization is renowned for recruiting top talent from prestigious Ivy League institutions—highly skilled researchers, engineers, and scientists tasked with advancing science, aeronautics, and space exploration for the benefit of humanity. While this ambitious mission drives the organization, they often expect their employees to embody the vision—and as individual contributors, they usually do. The organization frequently assumes that past achievements signal readiness for leadership roles.

Take Luke, for example, a highly successful electrical engineer who had been with the company for 12 years. He had worked on numerous highprofile projects and earned a solid reputation as an expert in power system design, contributing significantly to energy storage and power generation efforts for the Gateway and Orion projects. With the pressure of the Mars 2024 initiative looming, his team was under strict deadlines to deliver their designs on time and within budget, and he rose to the occasion.

Luke was recently promoted to supervisor within the Electrical Division. While he was technically proficient, this was his first leadership role. Eager to make a difference, he began meeting with his team, offering suggestions on how their processes could be improved. However, after a few months, Luke noticed that productivity and engagement were declining—employees even began avoiding him. Ultimately, Luke took an internal course called *Transitioning from Peer to Supervisor*, focusing on acknowledging the transition, establishing credibility, building rapport with the team, clarifying expectations, and managing conflict.

Luke began to utilize the tools and information from the training and saw an increase in his team's engagement.

Lessons from the Trenches

- **Lesson:** Employees on the frontlines often have a deep understanding of the customer experience, operational inefficiencies, and potential improvements.

- **Impact:** Leveraging this knowledge can help leaders make more informed decisions and improve processes.

- **Lesson:** Effective leaders show understanding and consideration for their team members' feelings and perspectives. They recognize that employees are human beings with unique needs, and they act with compassion.

- **Lesson:** Empathy builds trust and fosters a supportive environment, making employees feel seen, valued, and understood.

For Reflection:

Defining your identity as a new leader is crucial, and fostering strong working relationships will be key to thriving in your new role. These questions are designed to guide your reflection on your leadership style and values, helping you find the right balance between management and leadership.

1. What motivated you to pursue leadership? What are your goals, ambitions, and reasons for stepping into this role?

2. What core values guide you as both a leader and an individual?

3. How would you characterize your leadership style? How do you think others would describe it?

4. How can you effectively balance both management and leadership skills in your new position?

CHAPTER 2

The Humble Leader: Tame Your Ego

The first half of life is devoted to forming a healthy ego, the second half is going inward and letting go of it.

~ Carl Jung, Swiss psychiatrist and psychotherapist

Growing up, my grandmother often reminded us, "Don't be a showoff," or "No one likes a know-it-all." These phrases were her way of teaching us to manage our egos and behave appropriately in social settings. So, what exactly is ego? Austrian neurologist Sigmund Freud, who has made significant contributions to the study of the ego, describes it as a part of our personality that emerges during adolescence (Freud, 1989). It is at this stage that children begin to develop their own identity and gradually separate themselves from parental or authoritative figures. According to Freud (1989), the ego consists of three parts:

- **The Id:** The instinctual component of the psyche that desires immediate satisfaction, often acting without regard for logic or reason.

- **The Superego:** The moral compass that governs the id, focused on societal norms and the pursuit of ideal standards.

- **The Ego:** The mediator between the id and superego, maintaining a balanced approach that avoids impulsiveness or excessive rigidity.

This raises the question: Is ego inherently bad? The answer is no. The ego is an essential part of who we are. According to psychologist Kendra Cherry (2024), the ego represents a combination of our values, preferences, and assumptions, shaping our unique identity.

However, problems arise when the ego becomes unbalanced, and either the id or the superego takes over. If the id dominates, individuals may behave recklessly, disregarding others in their pursuit of instant gratification. In today's workplace, we see this manifested when people lose their temper in meetings, seek power at any cost, refuse to accept criticism or take credit for others' work. They often have an inflated sense of their abilities and overestimate their competence.

On the other hand, if the superego prevails, individuals set overly high standards for themselves and others. This can result in behaviors like constantly seeking approval, being excessively self-critical, procrastinating, or becoming obsessed with how others perceive them.

When the id and superego are balanced, the ego acts as a mediator, maintaining a healthy equilibrium that avoids impulsiveness and rigidity. As Cam Snaith (2020) explains in *Taming Your Ego*, the relationship with the ego is complex. The more we learn to control our egos, the less we feel the need to dominate every situation, seek validation, or conform to others' expectations. Taming our ego is a crucial step toward becoming more effective leaders.

The Link Between Humility and the Ego

Humility and ego are closely intertwined. Researchers Joseph Chancellor and Sonja Lyubomirsky (2013) pointed out that humility is often one of the most neglected and underappreciated virtues. Despite being one of the least studied leadership qualities, it has gained more attention from researchers in recent years.

Humility finds its place within the ego, existing in the space between the id and the superego. It can be viewed as a spectrum—ranging from pretentiousness to balanced humility to modesty.

- **Pretentiousness—which is linked to the id**—exhibits an inflated sense of self-importance, disregards others' perspectives, and refuses to recognize personal limitations.

- **Balanced humility—which is linked the ego**—reflects selfassurance, an acceptance of one's limitations, openness, and a belief in equality.

- **Modesty—which is linked the superego**—undervaluing one's skills and abilities and displaying a lack of confidence.

Being humble involves having a clear and realistic understanding of oneself, others, and the world.

Humble Leadership

Humble leadership has gained significant attention in the 21st century and intersects with other leadership theories, such as transformational, authentic, servant, and inclusive leadership. According to Bradley Owens and fellow researchers, humility in leadership is a people-focused approach where leaders possess self-awareness, recognize the strengths and contributions of others, and remain open to new ideas and feedback (Owens et al., 2013). Their research shows that humble leadership enhances employee job satisfaction and engagement, as employees feel acknowledged, valued, and heard by such leaders.

However, as individuals climb the organizational ladder, gaining more authority, titles, or status, their egos can inflate, often leading to a breakdown in trust between them and their subordinates. In fact, the higher leaders rise and become distanced from day-to-day tasks, the more they need to rely on those who are immersed in the work. Leaders would benefit from actively seeking employee input on processes, new products, and initiatives before making decisions that directly impact their teams, the customer experience, and the organization's success.

By cultivating a culture rooted in trust and humility rather than power and control, leaders encourage employees to bring their best selves to work and consistently exceed expectations. Conversely, a culture dominated by power and coercion fosters fear, undermining motivation, creativity, and learning. Adopting a humble leadership style—which combines humility, courage, and a willingness to leverage the collective experience of the team rather than relying solely on their own insight—creates a collaborative atmosphere. Leadership experts like Israel Sánchez-Cardona and other fellow researchers suggest that humble leaders inspire their teams to share, refine, and integrate knowledge through collaboration, driving the organization toward optimal solutions (Sánchez-Cardona et al., 2018). Dan Cable, writing for Harvard Business

Review, adds that humble leaders also foster creativity and ownership by empowering employees to experiment with new ideas and take responsibility for their actions and decisions (Cable, 2018).

Joseph Chancellor and Sonja Lyubomirsky (2013) argue that humility can be developed and nurtured. Leaders must be willing to acknowledge their limitations, model a willingness to learn, and highlight the strengths and contributions of their teams. This approach positively impacts employees' attitudes toward their leader, enhancing outcomes such as job satisfaction, engagement, and psychological safety.

As leadership expert John Maxwell (2007) aptly stated, leadership is fundamentally about influence. Without the ability to inspire others to follow, one cannot truly be considered a leader. Maxwell (2007) explains that influence is built on a leader's character—traits like trustworthiness, integrity, and humility—along with their ability to foster positive relationships throughout the organization, their knowledge, experience, and proven track record. All of these factors play a crucial role in whether others choose to follow them.

Lessons from the Trenches

Michael was the owner and founder of a small family-run business specializing in custom and movable glass and wall panels. Howard, an employee, recalled that when he first started at the company, he often saw a small-statured man sweeping and mopping the shop floor. This man was friendly, greeting employees every morning. Howard assumed he was a janitor until one day, he asked a colleague, "Who's the guy with the broom?" To his surprise, the response was, "That's the owner."

As a newcomer, Howard was struck by Michael's humility—how the owner took pride in keeping the workplace clean, connected with employees, sought their input, and recognized their contributions. When the company lost its only salesperson, Michael personally returned to the road to handle sales himself, a logical step given his deep product knowledge and established industry reputation. Meanwhile, he promoted his son-in-law, Matthew, to Chief Operating Officer (COO) to oversee daily operations. However, Matthew's leadership style contrasted sharply with Michael's—he was more reserved, seldom engaged with employees, and was quick to criticize their work. As a result, the workplace atmosphere took a downturn, only improving when Michael was present.

With his promotion to COO, Matthew's ego seemed to inflate. He began altering long-standing work practices and implementing new procedures. One day, Michael approached Howard and asked, "Why are you doing it this way?" Howard replied, "Matthew told me to." Michael brought Matthew over and asked why he had instructed Howard to wire the wall that way. Rather than reprimand Matthew, Michael patiently explained the original wiring process and why it gave them a competitive edge. He also encouraged Howard to speak up if he felt certain directions were counterproductive or not in the organization's best interest.

Michael embodied humble leadership. He held both himself and his team accountable, owned his mistakes, and forgave others. He fostered a psychologically safe environment where employees felt empowered, even encouraged, to express differing opinions. Above all, he celebrated the company's successes and shared the rewards with his employees.

Lessons from the Trenches

- **Lesson:** Employees appreciate leaders who are humble, open to feedback, and willing to learn from their team.

- **Impact:** Humility helps leaders build stronger connections, foster a culture of mutual respect, and create a more collaborative environment.

- **Lesson:** Employees respect leaders who "walk the talk." When leaders demonstrate the values and work ethic they expect from their team, it sets a standard for behavior.

- **Impact:** This consistency creates a culture of integrity and motivates employees to mirror those positive behaviors.

For Reflection:

Individuals should lead with humility and empathy, fostering a wellbalanced and healthy sense of self. These questions are designed to encourage deeper reflection on how humility plays a role in your leadership approach and how it can be nurtured within your team and organization.

1. In what ways do you demonstrate humility in your daily leadership interactions?

2. How might your ego interfere with your leadership?

3. How do you handle feedback or criticism, especially when it challenges your ideas or decisions?

4. When was the last time you admitted a mistake or showed vulnerability to your team? How did it impact the team dynamic?

CHAPTER 3 Mastering the Art of Connection

I've learned that people will forget what you said, people will forget what you did, but people will never forget how you made them feel.

~ Maya Angelou, American poet

People are inherently social; we seek out connection and supportive interactions just as we need food and water. Stronger relationships in the work environment contribute to greater happiness, well-being, and productivity. However, not everyone finds building relationships natural or easy to do. Even those who are naturally charismatic can benefit from refining their abilities in this area.

In this chapter, we will explore key strategies that help leaders foster positive workplace relationships, showing care for their colleagues while maintaining a focus on achieving results

The Power of Trust

Employees crave authentic connections with their leaders. When employees can trust their leaders and believe that their leaders care about them, then they feel a greater sense of loyalty—which increases productivity and retention. Patrick Lencioni (2010), author, noted that trust lies at the heart of a functioning, cohesive team. Without it, teamwork is all but impossible.

Leaders must cultivate trust by engaging in open communication with their teams, sharing experiences, fostering an environment where team members feel comfortable with each other, and upholding their credibility.

Whether you are building a relationship with a senior leader, colleague, or employee, success hinges on trust, respect, and understanding—and requires continuous effort from both sides. According to Roger Mayer and other researchers, trust is the key driver in strengthening relationships and encouraging vulnerability between individuals (Mayer et al., 1995). When challenges emerge, they should be addressed directly and professionally to ensure the relationship continues to evolve and improve.

In *The Speed of Trust,* Stephen M. R. Covey (2006) emphasized that trust is not an intangible or elusive trait that people either possess or lack. Instead, it is a practical, measurable, and actionable asset that can be developed more quickly than most people realize. Drs. Dennis and Michelle Reina (2009) of the Trust Building Institute have outlined three essential components of trust-building, along with their corresponding behaviors.

1. **Credibility** – A leader's capability to fulfill their responsibilities.

   Key behaviors include setting clear expectations, defining boundaries, effective delegation, honoring commitments, and demonstrating consistency.

2. **Integrity** – A leader's dependability in following through on their promises.

   Integrity is exhibited through behaviors such as transparent communication, truthfulness in challenging situations, acknowledging mistakes, offering and accepting constructive feedback, safeguarding confidentiality, and assuming positive intent.

3. **Leadership** – A leader's expressions of care, compassion, and empathy toward employees and the employee's reciprocation.

   Leadership is reflected in behaviors like showing empathy while ensuring accountability, recognizing employees' talents and skills, involving them in decision-making, and supporting their learning and development.

Establishing trust is the first step in building effective relationships. When people trust one another, have confidence in leadership, and have a clear goal, they can be highly productive.

Building Relationships

Authentic connections are essential. Although it may be tempting to maximize time by staying in your office, focused solely on work, leaders must move beyond their routines and be fully present. By staying attuned to employees' needs, desires, and aspirations, leaders can form stronger connections.

For some introverted or technically oriented leaders, building deep connections with employees may be challenging due to a natural inclination toward tasks over personal interaction. Technical leaders often prioritize getting the job done over getting to know their team on a personal level—their preferences, values, and goals. However, it is vital for leaders to connect with employees beyond work-related matters in areas such as their interests, life events, and values.

This level of connection requires leaders to embrace vulnerability by sharing their own experiences, successes, and failures. Vulnerability is the foundation of meaningful relationships. Anne M. Mulcahy, former chairperson and CEO of Xerox Corporation, observed, "Employees who believe that management cares about them as individuals—not just as workers—are more productive, satisfied, and fulfilled" (Amalia, 2021).

In some organizations, leaders may reduce their workforce to numbers, titles, or roles, ignoring the fact that each employee is an individual with a name and unique talents. Leaders who appreciate each person's distinct abilities and contributions show a deep level of care. By investing time to understand their employees personally, these leaders demonstrate empathy and help guide their team toward success. They recognize their employees' strengths and areas for improvement while continuously encouraging them to grow.

Additionally, leaders must recognize their employees' preferred ways of connecting. Several approaches can help leaders foster personal relationships with their teams:

- **Schedule time for personal conversations:** Take time to get to know each employee on a deeper level. A saying often attributed to Theodore Roosevelt is, "People don't care how much you know until they know how much you care."

- **Adopt an open-door policy:** This applies both literally and figuratively. Having your door open signals approachability, while metaphorically, it assures employees that their concerns are welcome and not seen as an inconvenience. Make time for their questions and address issues promptly.

- **Increase engagement:** Make it a habit to walk around the office, engaging with employees on both professional and personal matters.

- **Be transparent:** Employees value leaders who are honest, admit their mistakes, and readily share information.

- **Get involved:** Leaders must demonstrate and model a strong work ethic. Show a willingness to work alongside your team, whether it is tackling difficult challenges together or motivating them to achieve major milestones.

- **Exchange feedback:** Offer regular feedback to employees and be open to receiving it as well. Leaders should act as coaches who guide and motivate employees toward their full potential.

- **Practice gratitude:** Show appreciation for your employees' efforts in achieving organizational goals. Gratitude strengthens relationships and reinforces positive behavior.

Lessons from the Trenches

Nicole was a collection specialist, who worked for five years at a national bank in Cleveland, OH. During this time, she experienced frequent turnovers in leadership and among her colleagues. Then, the bank hired an Employee Engagement Manager named Marie to develop a program focused on attracting, developing, and retaining talent. On Marie's first day, she walked through the office and took the time to personally connect with each employee. Nicole shared how Marie approached her, asking what she enjoyed most about working in collections, what challenges she faced, and—most importantly—inquiring about her personal life.

Marie noticed a picture of Nicole's dog and asked questions about it, which led Nicole to reveal that just two weeks prior, she had lost her dog, Spikey. Nicole was deeply touched by Marie's thoughtfulness and genuine interest in something so personal.

Marie did not stop there. She spent the entire day engaging in similar conversations with the rest of the 18-member team, making it a priority to get to know everyone. The next day, she repeated the process— greeting each employee and checking in with them. Nicole reflected that no previous supervisor had ever taken the time to get to know the employees. They were typically judged by the amount of money they recovered. Although the top collector would receive special recognition, personal connections were absent. Nicole even mentioned that her own supervisor did not know about Spikey's passing. When asked why she didn't share this with him, Nicole simply replied, "He does not care."

When asked what stood out most about Marie's actions, Nicole highlighted three key things:

- First, Marie's actions were more than just a kind gesture. She made it a habit to walk the floor each morning before starting her work, engaging in sincere and authentic conversations. Even if she was busy with meetings, she made sure to connect with the team at some point throughout the day.

- Second, Marie shared details about her own life, including her family, her past experiences, and lessons learned. This personal transparency helped her connect with each employee on a deeper level. She remembered important details like birthdays and weddings and made it a point to acknowledge them in meaningful ways.

- Lastly, Marie involved the employees in the process of developing the new engagement program. She sought their ideas and then demonstrated that she valued their input by incorporating many of their suggestions into the overall plan.

Nicole's story highlights the profound impact a leader can have on how employees perceive both leadership and the organization as a whole. When employees feel that their leaders genuinely care about them, it builds loyalty, strengthens relationships, fosters collaboration, and boosts morale, productivity, and a sense of community.

Lessons from the Trenches

- **Lesson**: Sharing personal stories or being open about challenges fosters authenticity. Vulnerability creates a safe space for others to share their experiences, leading to more meaningful connections.

- **Impact:** This deepens trust and paves the way for more genuine relationships, which can inspire creativity, collaboration, and personal growth.

- **Lesson:** Leaders who master connection are better able to inspire, motivate, and influence others.

- **Impact:** These behaviors enhance productivity, and morale, and create a sense of community, leading to high retention rates and increased productivity.

For Reflection:

Developing strong connections is an essential leadership skill. The following questions are intended to prompt thoughtful consideration of the leader's role in fostering positive relationships with their team:

1. How do you typically form connections with others?

2. Reflect on a recent conversation with an employee where you truly listened to their story. What insights did you gain about that person? What did you learn about yourself? How did this affect your relationship?

3. How can you tell when a strong relationship and trust have been established?

4. What actions or behaviors have you noticed that help cultivate trust?

CHAPTER 4 Uncharted Territory

The task of the leader is to get his people from where they are to where they have not been.

~ Henry Kissinger, former U.S. National Security Advisor & Secretary of State

In today's fast-paced world, organizations must be more adaptable than ever, not just to survive but to thrive and grow. External forces often push companies to break away from the status quo. Author Denise Morgan notes that such pressures can come from globalization, advancing technologies, competitor's actions, customer and partner insights, digitization, ecommerce, social media, and shifts in the political, economic, cultural, or technological landscapes (Morgan, 2018). These external forces are often summarized by the military acronym VUCA—volatility, uncertainty, complexity, and ambiguity—a term coined in the late 1990s to describe the increasingly unpredictable and rapidly changing business environment (Abidi & Joshi, 2015). Simply put, VUCA has become the new normal, characterizing the chaos and turbulence of modern industries.

To navigate this VUCA world, leaders must establish a clear and compelling vision and communicate it effectively throughout their organizations. This requires strategic foresight and an actionable plan to address ongoing challenges. Additionally, organizations need to foster an agile workforce capable of swiftly adapting both people and processes in response to the problems and opportunities that arise.

In this chapter, we will delve into how leaders can craft visionary goals, conduct strategic planning, manage large-scale transformations, and inspire creativity and innovation within their teams.

Vision & Strategic Thinking

Leaders play a pivotal role in setting the direction of an organization. Visionary leaders inspire their teams with a powerful sense of mission, guiding them toward shared goals while providing the knowledge and skills needed for success. This approach enhances overall organizational performance. Visionary leaders articulate a clear and compelling vision for the future, motivate employees to achieve it, and foster a positive work environment. Think of leaders like Steve Jobs, who revolutionized technology with Apple; Elon Musk, who disrupted industries with innovations in transportation, energy, and space; Oprah Winfrey, who transformed the television industry; Martin Luther King Jr., who galvanized a generation with his "I Have a Dream" speech; and Indra Nooyi, who redefined PepsiCo's culture by promoting healthier products and sustainability. What unites these leaders is their visionary approach.

A vision, as defined by the Oxford Dictionary, is the ability to imagine or plan for the future with creativity or wisdom. Visionary leaders possess this ability, crafting a vivid picture of the future and translating it into actionable steps for their followers. These leaders communicate their vision both through words and actions, making it clear what needs to be done to bring the vision to life. People tend to think in pictures, so the vision must be concrete and focused on a higher purpose. If followers sense that the vision is self-serving, they are less likely to embrace it and more likely to maintain the status quo.

Visionary leaders are forward-thinking and innovative. They see the bigger picture and create a compelling vision that challenges the current norms, reshapes industries, or introduces groundbreaking products and services. Their ambition to effect positive change drives them to envision a future that does not yet exist.

A *Harvard Business Review* article on visionary leadership points out that while having a vision is essential, leaders must also secure buy-in, particularly from middle managers, to ensure the vision becomes a reality (Ates et al., 2019). Larry Lashway (1997), the author of *Leading with Vision*, asserts that a vision is more than feel-good rhetoric, mission statements, or strategic plans; it should engage people, give meaning to their work, set a high standard of excellence, and link the present to the future.

James Kouzes and Barry Posner (2006), authors of *The Leadership Challenge*, offer a process for inspiring a shared vision. They suggest that visionary leaders scan the external environment to anticipate future trends and develop a forward-looking perspective on what the organization can become. The vision must be rooted in a common purpose that resonates with employees. While leaders should present a vivid picture of the future, employees also must be able to see themselves in it.

To secure greater employee commitment, leaders should involve their teams in the vision-creation process. The vision should be optimistic and centered on a shared objective. Leaders must listen closely to their employees, understand their aspirations, and merge them with the organizational goals to create a unified vision for the future. When employees see how their roles contribute to the vision, it motivates them to work toward the common goal. According to Motivating Language Theory, developed by Jeremiah Sullivan, leaders who use versatile language are better able to engage, motivate, and build commitment among their followers, leading to improved organizational performance (Sullivan, 1988).

Moreover, the vision itself must be compelling. Kouzes and Posner (2006) argue that symbolic language should be used to evoke emotions and foster a sense of community. It should incorporate imagery that helps employees visualize the organization's future. The vision should also be optimistic, which can instill greater confidence and resilience in the workforce. Leaders must communicate with passion, sincerity, and energy to increase the likelihood that the collective vision will succeed.

Strategic Planning

While an organizational vision outlines a future of possibilities, strategic planning provides the roadmap to transition from the present state to that envisioned future. Typically, organizations turn to strategic planning when internal or external pressures become too intense, compelling a change in direction. Strategic planning, therefore, serves as the driving force that propels organizations forward.

Organizations of all sizes engage in strategic planning, tailoring it to fit their complexity and business model. George A. Steiner (2010), author of *Strategic Planning*, distinguishes between two types of planning: operational and strategic. Operational planning centers on day-to-day activities, often within a one-year timeframe. In contrast, Steiner (2010) emphasized that strategic planning must encompass three key elements: (1) a forward-looking orientation, (2) a structured process, and (3) a mindset or way of thinking embedded in the organization.

S.K. Bhattacharyya (1972), a researcher, highlights three distinct activities within formal planning: (1) strategic planning to determine long-term objectives, (2) action planning for measuring and coordinating the strategic goals, and (3) operational planning, which focuses on shorter-term targets and performance.

Unfortunately, many organizations concentrate heavily on near-term forecasting and operational trends while often neglecting strategic foresight, such as scenario planning. Unlike strategic planning, which generally covers a 1- to 5-year horizon, scenario planning looks further ahead, considering longer-term implications beyond the 5-year mark. Thomas J. Chermack (2011), an expert in organizational performance, notes that while traditional strategic planning has provided some insights for navigating a rapidly changing environment, it often falls short in anticipating political, environmental, economic, or societal shifts.

Futurist Richard Slaughter (1997) defines strategic foresight as the ability to develop a coherent and actionable vision of the future that can be leveraged for organizational advantage. Similarly, futurist James Canton

41

(2015) emphasizes that "Being future-smart" enables individuals and organizations to anticipate trends that could transform markets, innovations, and workforces.

Virginia Richardson (2020), an adjunct professor at Regent University, explains that scenario planning examines multiple plausible futures by employing strategic foresight tools such as STEEPLE (social, technical, economic, environmental, political, legal, and ethical factors). Unlike strategic planning, which tends to focus on predictable outcomes, scenario planning encourages organizations to explore uncertainties or potential blind spots that could impact their business over the next 5, 10, or even 20 years (Richardson, 2020).

Chermack (2011) outlines a five-phase framework for scenario planning that organizations can adopt:

1. **Project Preparation**: Define the purpose, scope, timeframe, and outcomes.

2. **Scenario Exploration**: Conduct external analysis using tools like STEEPLE.

3. **Scenario Development**: Identify major forces, uncertainties, and potential impacts.

4. **Scenario Implementation**: Test business strategies against developed scenarios.

5. **Project Assessment**: Evaluate the performance and outcomes.

By incorporating scenario planning, organizations gain a deeper understanding of external influences, develop innovative solutions to challenges, and create more resilient strategies that align with their operational systems. Those who engage in long-term scenario planning are better equipped to navigate future uncertainties and changes that occur over the next 10 to 20 years.

Not all organizations embrace strategic planning effectively. Victor Cascella (2002), president of Niscient Inc., argues that poor strategic planners often fail to align strategy across all levels of the organization, leading to resource misallocation and inadequate operational measures. To avoid these pitfalls, Cascella (2002) recommends defining the organization's core processes that deliver value to customers, identifying which aspects of those processes contribute most to strategic goals, and encouraging employees to propose and implement improvements that offer a competitive advantage.

Large Scale Change Initiatives

Organizations may have a compelling vision and invest time in strategic planning, but without effectively managing large-scale change, they risk losing their ability to adapt to shifting markets and both internal and external pressures, potentially compromising their competitiveness. Various models exist to guide organizations through substantial transformations, such as mergers, technology adoption, cost reductions, downsizing, and cultural shifts.

The success of these change efforts often depends on the organization's ability to navigate cultural challenges. Every organization has a unique culture shaped by deeply held beliefs, values, and established practices. Researcher Kay Dennis (2016) points out that leaders create the conditions for culture, managers maintain and monitor it, and employees embody it daily. A culture that embraces innovation and challenges the status quo—grounded in a supportive mindset and strong leadership—is key to effective change management.

Before initiating any change, leaders must assess the potential impact on their workforce. According to McKinsey senior partners Scott Keller and Bill Schaninger (2019), organizations are six times more likely to succeed in change initiatives if they take employee mindsets into account. Organizations that are resistant to change often cling to traditional practices and policies, limiting their ability to innovate and grow despite mounting external pressures.

This makes it crucial for leaders to evaluate their organization's readiness for change. Here are some questions leaders might ask to gauge whether their organization is prepared:

- How well-equipped is the organization to absorb the planned changes without overwhelming key areas?

- What skills, experience, and resources must be in place to support the change?

- Is leadership capable of effectively sponsoring and championing the change?

- What drives a desire for change, and where might resistance arise?

- What steps can be taken to enhance support and minimize obstacles?

- How has the organization historically managed change, and what aspects of the corporate culture might help or hinder this effort?

Successful organizational change heavily depends on a leader's ability to shift employee mindsets. Researchers like Lorenzo Duchi argue that mindsets, whether growth-oriented (believing the world is adaptable and can change) or fixed (seeing the world as static and unchanging), play a major role in shaping responses to change (Duchi et al., 2020).

Employees often resist change for several reasons, as identified by psychologist A.J. Schuler (2003), including viewing change as a risk, attachment to old ways of doing things, lack of role models for the new approach, perceived incompetence in adapting, feeling overwhelmed, fear of loss of status or quality of life, or a genuine belief that the new ideas are flawed.

Being deliberate and proactive in addressing these challenges involves setting clear goals, intervening appropriately to guide the change, and holding employees accountable to new norms. Just as important as the change itself are the leaders guiding the process. They must navigate diverse interests from employees, customers, and stakeholders, all of whom can influence the outcome of any change effort.

Henry Mintzberg (1975), a Canadian author, identifies three key roles for leaders during change: interpersonal, informational, and decisional. Effective leaders should possess a charismatic presence that attracts rather than alienates, and they should build strong relationships with everyone involved in the change effort (Mintzberg, 1975). Trust and credibility are paramount, as employees need to believe their leader genuinely cares about both the workforce and the overall success of the organization (Mintzberg, 1975).

Leaders must also be the voice of change, articulating its urgency and impact on both the organization and its employees. By generating shortterm wins, celebrating progress, empowering employees to take action, and embedding the change into the culture, leaders build momentum for lasting transformation.

Additionally, leaders must serve as decision-makers, innovators, resource allocators, and chief negotiators. Change efforts are likely to fail if critical elements are missing, such as a clear need for the change, a compelling vision, adequate training, incentives, and resources, and a solid plan. For instance, if leaders fail to communicate the urgency of change, the status quo will prevail. If vision is lacking, confusion will follow. If employees are not properly trained, anxiety will increase. Without sufficient resources or a plan, frustration will undermine the effort.

Change is rarely a straightforward, linear process with a clear beginning and end; it is ongoing. High-performing organizations are those that continuously evaluate and adjust their strategies, measuring success based on performance outcomes, employee behavior, and productivity. Tools like internal surveys and employee engagement data can offer valuable insights, helping leaders determine whether their change strategy is on track or if adjustments are needed.

Creativity & Innovation

Part of a leader's role in exploring uncharted territory is to foster a culture that encourages creativity and innovation. Creativity is often seen as the foundational element of innovation. According to David Hughes and his colleagues, creativity, and innovation in the workplace are reflected through the processes, outcomes, and products that arise from efforts to develop and implement new and improved methods (Hughes et al, 2018). David O'Sullivan and Lawrence Dooley (2008), authors of *Applying Innovation*, describe creativity as the cognitive process that generates practical, actionable, and novel ideas, while innovation transforms the results of the creative process into value by refining and developing them.

Some researchers distinguish creativity as an internal process, with innovation being the external execution. Creativity involves generating fresh, applicable ideas—such as introducing new methods, techniques, or processes into the organization. Innovation, on the other hand, takes these ideas and develops them further, requiring resources such as time, money, equipment, and, crucially, human talent.

Hughes and his colleagues (2018) emphasize that creativity is the initial phase of this journey, focusing on generating ideas, while innovation involves the actualization of those ideas into improved procedures, practices, or products. Innovation represents the second stage, where concepts are turned into reality through production and execution.

A recent McKinsey & Company survey found that 70 percent of senior executives believe innovation will be one of the top three drivers of growth for their companies over the next three to five years (Heim, 2017). Many see innovation as the key to accelerating the pace of change in today's global business landscape.

Leaders who instill an innovation mindset within their organizations need to be visionary, identify growth opportunities, establish principles that challenge conventional thinking, and maintain a positive outlook. Creating an environment that embraces disruption can yield innovative products and services, driving profitability. Jack Welch, the former CEO of General Electric, once said, "My job is to listen to, search for, and spread ideas, to expose people to good ideas. When self-confident people see a good idea, they love it" (Welch et al., 1993).

George Llopis (2017), author of *The Innovation Mentality*, outlines several strategies for cultivating an innovation mindset within organizations:

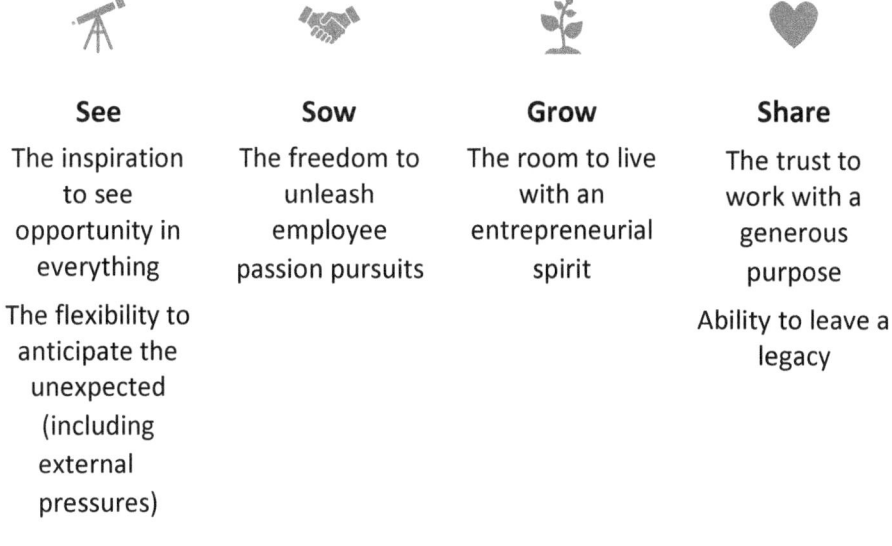

See	Sow	Grow	Share
The inspiration to see opportunity in everything	The freedom to unleash employee passion pursuits	The room to live with an entrepreneurial spirit	The trust to work with a generous purpose
The flexibility to anticipate the unexpected (including external pressures)			Ability to leave a legacy

Consider the case of 3M, a company renowned for its innovation and iconic products, including masking tape, Post-It Notes, and Scotchgard. The 3M leadership team has cultivated an environment where innovative ideas are encouraged and transformed into successful products. In their book *Applying Innovation*, O'Sullivan and Dooley (2008) highlighted several key policies, processes, and practices that have contributed to 3M's success:

- **Intentional recruitment of creative, independent thinkers** with specialized expertise to support each division.

- A company ethos of "Better to ask for forgiveness than permission" which **empowers employees to pursue their ideas** even if they lack immediate approval from supervisors.

- The **15% rule** allows employees to dedicate up to 15% of their time to exploring innovative projects that could benefit the company. This flexibility fosters experimentation and leads to discoveries with commercial potential.

- A target of **30% of annual revenue** must come from products less than four years old, ensuring that employees continuously innovate rather than relying on past successes.

- Ongoing investment in **training and development**, enabling all employees to maximize their contributions to the company's long-term sustainability.

Innovative leadership is essential for driving organizational growth, creativity, and effectiveness. Leaders play a crucial role in building a culture of innovation, guiding employees and stakeholders through the development process, and ensuring successful implementation. As former Supreme Court Justice Oliver Wendell Holmes once said, "Once a new idea has stretched the mind, it never returns to its original dimensions."

Lessons from the Trenches

In response to the 2021 Presidential Executive Order aimed at transforming the federal customer experience and service delivery to restore trust in government, many federal agencies began seeking ways to streamline internal processes. A government agency took this opportunity to evaluate its administrative support functions. With the post-pandemic transition to a hybrid work environment, the roles of administrative professionals shifted significantly. Tasks such as answering phones and serving as gatekeepers outside supervisors' offices were no longer central responsibilities. Therefore, the agency tasked a study team with reassessing the roles of administrative assistants and officers in this new hybrid context.

As a result, the agency consolidated all administrative services into a unified department called the Office of Administrative Services, encompassing administrative assistants, officers, and a business unit for handling credit card purchases. This restructuring centralized the administrative workforce under new leadership, with the newly formed office comprising 40% civil servants and 60% contractors.

At the same time, the contract for administrative services was being recompeted, which led to significant upheaval for employees and contractors alike. The award of a new contract resulted in job losses, reduced pay and benefits, and a drop in morale.

The consolidation led to organizational disruption. Before the change, administrative professionals were decentralized, reporting directly to their supervisors within various directorates, divisions, or branches. Each unit had its own distinct work processes, and administrative staff were deeply embedded in their respective organizational cultures, many having served between 15 and 30 years. Following the transition, the organization experienced a loss of approximately 40% of contractor staff and 35% of civil servant staff, further exacerbating low morale and trust. Retaining the remaining administrative workforce became a pressing challenge.

Interviews with staff revealed several key issues with the change process:

- **Lack of a clear vision and implementation plan:** Simultaneous large-scale changes—the creation of the Office of Administrative Services and a contract changeover—left the environment dynamic and unstable. Expectations and guidelines constantly shifted, and roles and responsibilities were unclear. Communication from leadership was delayed, leaving affected employees little time to provide input or prepare for the changes.

- **Lack of leadership:** Signs of change fatigue were overlooked by management, and a change champion was not appointed to guide the transition, resulting in confusion about decision-making and accountability.

- **No involvement in the decision-making process:** Branch and Division Chiefs were not consulted before the consolidation, limiting their ability to contribute to the implementation plan. Employees felt they were merely told what to do without being provided sufficient explanation for the change.

- **Lack of empathy for employees:** Employees felt disconnected from the change process and undervalued. Uncertainty about job security under the new contract further contributed to feelings of insecurity and dissatisfaction.

- **Lack of trust in leadership:** The lack of communication regarding the terms of the new contract led to suspicion among contractors, who felt the information was being withheld or distorted. Overall, trust in senior leadership diminished.

- **Role ambiguity:** Discontent over unclear roles and backup responsibilities persisted, with many employees finding it difficult to feel positive about new roles due to the general dissatisfaction among their colleagues.

Researcher Kay Dennis (2016) suggests that the most effective way to shift mindsets and drive successful change initiatives includes developing a compelling vision, involving employees in decision-making, and empowering them to execute change with autonomy. Encouraging innovative ideas, acknowledging the complexity of change, setting realistic goals, establishing performance measures, and celebrating successes—particularly behavioral changes—can help agencies recover from failed change initiatives (Dennis, 2016).

Implementing these strategies could help the government agency rebuild trust, improve morale, and ultimately succeed in its transformation efforts.

Lessons from the Trenches

- **Lesson:** Leaders with a clear vision and strategic mindset inspire employees by providing direction and purpose. They can articulate where the team or organization is headed and why.

- **Impact:** A clear vision motivates employees to align their efforts with the broader goals of the organization.

- **Lesson:** Leaders must be able to adapt quickly, innovate, and empower their teams to experiment and learn.

- **Impact:** When leaders openly acknowledge unknowns while encouraging calculated risk-taking, it creates a culture where employees feel safe to contribute ideas and challenge the status quo without fear of failure.

For Reflection:

Venturing into unknown territory can be a challenging endeavor for organizations. Leaders must possess the right skills to set visionary goals, engage in strategic planning, oversee significant transformations, and foster creativity and innovation within their teams. These questions help leaders maintain focus on key areas while adapting to a dynamic business environment.

1. How does the organization's vision for the future align with its core values and mission?

2. What actions can be taken to involve stakeholders in shaping and taking ownership of the organization's vision?

3. What internal and external factors are influencing the organization, and how can it proactively respond to these forces?

4. How prepared is the organization for the proposed change, and what potential risks need to be addressed?

5. How can leaders create a culture that encourages experimentation, risk-taking, and innovative thinking?

CHAPTER 5

Essential Communication:
The Key to Success and Collaboration

The art of communication is the language of leadership. ~
James C. Humes, author and former presidential speechwriter

Communication is a fundamental part of the human experience and serves as the foundation for building relationships and trust within an organization. As Professor Marigonë Krypa (2017) explains, the term communication originates from the Latin word *communis* or *commūnicāre*, meaning "To make common" or "To share." Krypa (2017) argues that communication is the process through which information, knowledge, and understanding are exchanged between individuals and offers an opportunity to express attitudes and opinions.

Leaders play a vital role in delivering key messages to their teams using mutually understood language, signs, and symbols. Communication flows in all directions within an organization—downward, upward, and laterally. Linguists Nurul Halima and Norizan Razak (2014) highlight three main purposes for communication within organizations: sharing information, motivating employees, and expressing emotion:

- **Information:** This involves disseminating facts, data, and instructions throughout the organization. A crucial component is the leader's ability to listen to diverse perspectives and integrate that feedback into decision-making.

- **Motivation:** Communication helps inspire employees to align with the organization's vision and mission. It clarifies roles, outlines expectations, and identifies the skills needed for success.

- **Emotional expression:** For many employees, the workplace is a key source of social interaction. Communication allows for the expression of feelings and the fulfillment of social needs while also enabling leaders to convey visions, goals, and values effectively.

As discussed in Chapter 4, leaders must foster meaningful, trust-based relationships with employees, and communication is the primary tool for doing so. By being open, sharing personal experiences, and showing vulnerability, leaders build trust with their teams.

Nonverbal communication is another crucial element of leadership. Employees are often attuned to both verbal and nonverbal signals. Nonverbal cues such as facial expressions, gestures, tone of voice, body language, personal space, and appearance play a significant role. Some researchers suggest that up to 80% of communication is conveyed through actions and gestures, with only 20% through words. When delivering important messages, employees may place more emphasis on a leader's nonverbal signals than the words themselves.

In this chapter, we will delve into the essentials of active listening, empathetic leadership, and the pivotal role storytelling plays in effective leadership.

Keys to Active Listening

Effective communication relies heavily on active listening, a skill many of us may not fully master. Active listening, which can be developed, shows genuine interest and respect for the speaker. Michael Hoppe, in his book *Active Listening: Improve Your Ability to Listen and Lead*, emphasizes that active listening involves paying close attention to what is being said by reflecting, understanding, clarifying, summarizing, and sharing information (Hoppe, 2016). This process requires both hearing the information (a physical act) and truly understanding it (a mental act).

You may have experienced distracted listening firsthand. For instance, imagine you're in a meeting with your supervisor, and midway through, they hear a ping from their phone and check the message. At that moment, they are no longer actively listening, as their focus has shifted. Active listening demands minimizing distractions, whether they are physical, like phones or computers, or mental, such as personal opinions, attitudes, or feelings about the speaker.

Other types of non-listening behaviors include pseudo-listening, selective listening, and defensive listening. Jovanovska (2021) explains that pseudo-listening happens when someone seems to be paying attention by nodding or occasionally asking questions, but their mind is elsewhere. Selective listening occurs when the listener only focuses on the parts of a conversation that interest them, ignoring the rest (Jovanovska, 2021). Defensive listening happens when the listener interprets information as a personal attack, causing them to become defensive (Jovanovska, 2021).

The International Listening Association (ILA) outlines several steps leaders can take to strengthen their listening skills:

1. Eliminate internal and external distractions, such as mobile phones.

2. Approach listening with an open mind.

3. Allow the speaker to finish before responding.

4. Pay attention to verbal and nonverbal cues indicating the importance of the message.

5. Listen for both emotional content and the meaning behind the words.

6. Be mindful of cultural, age, and gender differences that can affect how people communicate and listen.

7. Respond appropriately with verbal and non-verbal cues like asking questions, nodding, or making eye contact.

8. Clarify, summarize, and paraphrase to ensure accurate understanding.

9. Take appropriate action based on what you've heard.

Developing active listening skills is a clear indicator of a leader's communication competence—whether they can effectively convey information and listen to feedback. Active listening is an interactive process where both the speaker and listener engage in dialogue, using relevant verbal and non-verbal cues. This skill is essential for building relationships and fostering trust.

Communicating with Empathy

Empathy is a crucial element of effective communication. It involves the ability to understand another person's perspective and respond in a way that reflects that understanding. When leaders communicate with empathy, they help employees feel acknowledged, heard, and appreciated, affirming their viewpoints. Tzouramani (2017) highlights that "Research shows that empathetic leaders form emotional connections and are skilled at understanding and meeting the needs of their teams and customers.

They recognize others' talents, consider different perspectives in problemsolving, and involve people in decision-making" (p. 197).

Though sometimes viewed as a weakness, empathy is actually a sign of strength. It takes a confident and self-aware individual to listen to and understand diverse viewpoints while being open, transparent, and vulnerable. Leaders who practice empathy foster a workplace culture where empathy is shown by both leaders and employees regularly.

James Kouzes and Barry Posner, in *The Leadership Challenge*, assert that leaders who demonstrate empathy to their team members gain their commitment and buy-in, enhancing both productivity and engagement. Employees who feel supported and cared for are more willing to exceed expectations and are more open to a leader's influence (Kouzes & Posner, 2017).

While empathy cannot be taught directly, it can be developed through practice. It is shown through meaningful human interactions, where individuals make an intentional effort to see things from another's perspective, practice active listening, and respond with openness, transparency, and compassion.

Good Leaders Tell Stories

As discussed in Chapter 4, people naturally think in images, and storytelling is a powerful communication tool that allows leaders to create a vivid mental picture for their team.

For centuries, various cultures have passed down stories through generations as a way to connect, share information, and convey values and beliefs. Randee Lawrence & Dennis Paige (2016), authors of *What Our Ancestors Knew*, explain that storytelling has been a fundamental part of human culture since the earliest days—whether through cave paintings or gathering around fires. Stories serve as a way to share meaningful, timetested lessons and pass down personal and collective wisdom. Effective leaders use storytelling to enhance the messages they deliver.

Johnathan Clifton (2019), in *Investigating the Dark Side of Stories of 'Good' Leadership*, argues that storytelling helps leaders illustrate the success of their management and leadership philosophies, providing clear and relatable examples of good leadership. Gail Fairhurst (2007), a professor at the University of Cincinnati, adds that leaders often use stories to portray themselves as heroes or others as villains, painting a vivid picture to communicate their message effectively. Storytelling helps create a connection with others and leaves an immediate impact on listeners, allowing them to see themselves in the narrative and find meaning based on their perspectives.

Madeline Miles (2024), a writer and storyteller, defines storytelling as "the art of using language, vocalization, and physical movement and gesture to reveal the elements and images of a story to a specific audience." Maidhina K. Rahasya (2017), from the Indonesia University of Education, identified three key elements of storytelling: the setting, the listener, and the story itself. The setting can either enhance or detract from the story, while a smaller, more intimate environment allows for deeper engagement. The listener plays a crucial role, as they must be open to receiving the story's message. Lastly, the story should spark curiosity, serve a purpose, and teach a lesson, improving communication skills by using various language techniques to make it come alive.

Stories can be conveyed through diverse mediums such as spoken word, writing, film, music, or dance.

Consider some of today's great storytellers. Howard Schultz, for example, transformed Starbucks from a small coffee shop into a global brand by presenting it as a place where people could gather and connect (Louis, 2023). Richard Branson, known for his best-selling autobiographies *Losing My Virginity* and *The Virgin Way*, frequently shares his life experiences through interviews (Louis, 2023). Both Schultz and Branson are celebrated for their storytelling abilities, using empathy and emotional engagement to connect with people from all walks of life, helping them build global brands.

Michael Hackman and Craig Johnson (2013), in *Leadership: A Communication Perspective*, describe several purposes of storytelling: inspiring action, transmitting values, building a brand, fostering collaboration, quelling rumors, sharing knowledge, and leading people toward the future.

In summary, leaders who are effective communicators possess the ability to convey their ideas and information by actively listening, showing empathy, and telling compelling stories. The more leaders are willing to share and be vulnerable and transparent, the stronger the trust they build—leading to greater self-efficacy, employee productivity, and overall organizational success.

Lessons from the Trenches

On August 24, 2024, the National Aeronautics and Space Administration (NASA) held a press conference to address recent developments involving astronauts Suni Williams and Butch Wilmore, who were aboard the International Space Station due to leaks in the helium system of Boeing's Starliner, which pressurizes the spacecraft's thrusters. NASA Administrator Bill Nelson and his leadership team made the difficult decision to delay the astronauts' return, citing safety concerns and extending their stay in space until February 2025.

During the conference, Administrator Nelson, along with other NASA leaders, conveyed a message of openness and empathy, reiterating that safety remains the agency's core value. They acknowledged the emotional weight of past tragedies—Apollo I, Challenger, and Columbia—that claimed the lives of 17 astronauts, tapping into the collective sense of loss within NASA. The decision-making process was explained with transparency, underscoring the importance of balancing risk and innovation. Leaders encouraged employees to raise concerns or dissent, emphasizing the need for open dialogue within the agency. The team affirmed that the decision to prioritize astronaut safety was made unanimously.

Following the announcement, employees expressed appreciation for Nelson's leadership and the senior team's transparent communication. Their approach resonated with many, who found their remarks compelling due to: • Their emotional acknowledgment of past losses.

- Their clear reaffirmation of NASA's commitment to safety as its highest priority.

- Their thorough explanation of the decision-making process.

- Their encouragement for open communication and employee feedback.

- Their hopeful and optimistic vision for NASA's future.

Lessons from the Trenches

- **Lesson:** Clear, transparent, and consistent communication from leaders is crucial. Employees notice when leaders communicate expectations, provide feedback, and listen actively.

- **Impact:** Good communication prevents misunderstandings, aligns team goals, and encourages open dialogue.

- **Lesson:** Employees often highlight the impact of communication, whether it is the need for clarity in expectations or the importance of feedback.

> **Impact:** Leaders can refine their communication skills to ensure alignment, reduce misunderstandings, and foster a more collaborative environment.

For Reflection:

Effective communication is arguably one of the most vital skills for any leader. Use the following questions to evaluate both your own communication abilities and those of the leaders in your organization.

1. In what ways can leaders leverage communication to strengthen relationships, shape organizational culture, and drive ongoing engagement?

2. How does empathy influence a leader's approach to communication?

3. How do leaders incorporate active listening into their communication practices?

4. How can leaders create an environment where employees feel comfortable expressing differing opinions or raising concerns?

5. How can leaders in my organization communicate in a way that aligns with employees' values, concerns, and lived experiences?

CHAPTER 6 Distributed Power

Two heads are definitely better than one, and by sourcing ideas from each other, you have a better chance of coming up with a strategy that will allow your business to overcome a setback or challenge.

– Sir Richard Charles Nicholas Branson, Co-founder of Virgin Group

As employees advance within an organization, they often carry with them a mindset focused on completing tasks themselves. This can lead to micromanagement, with the belief that their way is the best or only way. However, as they transition from individual contributors to leadership roles, there is a realization that leaders cannot handle everything on their own and must depend on their teams to achieve organizational objectives. This shift highlights the critical importance of delegation as a core leadership skill. According to Baker and Murphy (2022), authors of *Delegation: A Core Leadership Skill*, delegation is the process by which a leader transfers responsibility for completing a task to another individual or group. Trusting team members with responsibilities and empowering them to make decisions is a hallmark of effective leadership. Leaders who delegate well demonstrate confidence in their team's abilities, which in turn fosters employee engagement and a sense of ownership, driving higher productivity and innovation.

In today's business environment, delegation and employee empowerment are increasingly important, particularly for early-career professionals. PwC's *Global Workforce Hopes and Fears Survey* (2022) revealed that
58% of Generation Zoomers and 63% of Millennials find it extremely or very important to have autonomy in how they approach their work, compared to 51% of Baby Boomers. Additionally, younger employees tend to view managers negatively if they do not provide sufficient autonomy. A Harvard Business Review article pointed out that "research shows that people have strong negative emotional and physiological

reactions to what they deem as unnecessary or unwanted help and that it can erode interpersonal relationships" (Fisher et al., 2021).

This chapter will explore the significance of delegation as a key leadership skill, offering strategies for leaders to delegate tasks effectively while avoiding common pitfalls in the process.

Situational Leadership

Situational Leadership, introduced by Paul Hersey and Kenneth Blanchard (1997), provides leaders with a framework for selecting directive or supportive behaviors based on an employee's readiness in specific situations. Rather than evaluating an employee's overall capability, this model encourages leaders to assess their developmental stage in relation to a particular task. Two key factors are considered: the employee's ability to perform the task (competence) and their confidence in doing so (commitment) (Hersey & Blanchard, 1997). Based on this assessment, leaders use more directive behaviors for employees who are less experienced or capable and supportive behaviors for those with higher maturity levels. Supportive behaviors include listening, offering encouragement, helping with problem-solving, and providing recognition, while directive behaviors involve setting clear goals, organizing tasks, communicating priorities, and establishing deadlines (Hersey & Blanchard, 1997). Leaders must adjust their approach depending on the situation, blending directive and supportive behaviors as necessary.

The Situational Leadership Model is divided into four leadership styles: telling, selling, participating, and delegating. These styles are based on the level of task direction and relationship support required, as well as the employee's readiness to take on the task (Hersey & Blanchard, 1997).

- **High-task, low-relationship** calls for more directive behavior, where leaders instruct employees on what, when, and how to complete tasks.

- **High-task, high-relationship** is known as selling, where leaders explain the reasoning behind the task, engaging employees in dialogue to gain their buy-in and support.

- **High-relationship, low-task** describes the participating style, where the employee is capable and knowledgeable enough to contribute to decision-making and take responsibility for completing the task.

- **Low-tasking and low-relationship refers to delegating, which is** the highest level of leadership. Here, employees are given full autonomy to carry out the task as they see fit, as they are both competent and motivated to take ownership and be accountable for the results.

Using the Situational Leadership Model helps distinguish between effective delegation and task dumping. It hinges on the employee's willingness to complete the task. Employees thrive when given meaningful work and the empowerment to execute it on their terms.

Conversely, if they feel micromanaged or stripped of decision-making power, frustration and dissatisfaction can lead to turnover.

When there's a mismatch between the employee's skills and the task, or when uninteresting tasks are assigned without authority, discretionary effort drops significantly. Drs. Edward Baker and Susan Murphy (2022) distinguish between delegation and dumping. They explain that "Delegating involves assigning tasks and responsibility to others while granting them the authority to make decisions. Dumping, on the other hand, is assigning mundane tasks without giving employees control over the process. This lack of authority leads to frustration, dissatisfaction, and eventually turnover" (p. 430). It is the leader's responsibility to ensure alignment between the task and the employee's abilities.

Employee Empowerment

Equally important to delegating tasks effectively is fostering a culture of empowerment. Empowerment centers on building trust between leaders and employees while creating an environment that promotes cooperation, team spirit, self-confidence, innovation, independent thinking, and entrepreneurial behavior (Elnaga & Imran, 2014).

Amir Elnaga and Amen Imran (2014) define empowerment as granting employees the autonomy and authority to make decisions, holding them accountable for their work, providing the necessary resources, and recognizing their efforts. Similarly, Sara Berraies and colleagues describe empowerment as a management approach that emphasizes employee autonomy, initiative, decentralization of power, and responsibility (Berraies et al., 2014). When organizations fully embrace empowerment, employees are more likely to exert discretionary effort—going above and beyond expectations—and experience greater job satisfaction. They become invested in their tasks and highly motivated to deliver their best work.

However, empowerment and delegation do not remove a leader's ultimate responsibility for the outcomes. Leaders remain accountable for ensuring their team meets its goals, but they shift into a role of motivation and guidance, overseeing employees without falling into micromanagement or adopting a hands-off approach.

Research indicates that empowered employees experience higher levels of job satisfaction and productivity (Elnaga & Imran, 2014). Other benefits include greater trust, reduced conflict, increased collaboration, lower turnover, and improved profitability (Elnaga & Imran, 2014).

Leaders must be confident enough in their own abilities to delegate authority to employees, involving them in decision-making and sharing the responsibility of achieving organizational goals. Some leaders may resist delegating power due to fears of losing control or status within the organization. The Society of Human Resource Management outlines several reasons leaders hesitate to delegate (Llyod, n.d.), including:

- The belief is that employees cannot perform tasks as well as the manager.
- The perception is that it is quicker to do the work themselves than to delegate.
- A lack of trust in employees' motivation or commitment to quality.
- A desire to feel indispensable.
- Simply enjoying the work themselves.

- Feeling guilty about giving more tasks to an already overworked team.

At the same time, giving too much autonomy can lead to arrogance or self-serving decisions that may not align with organizational goals. Leaders need to exercise discernment when distributing power, ensuring that employees chosen for increased responsibility are competent, emotionally mature, and capable of making sound decisions that benefit the organization.

Cultural Conditions

For a distributed power structure to function effectively, several key conditions must be present within an organization. M. Kemal Demġrcġ and Ali Erbaġ (2010) identified the following factors that foster a topdown approach to empowerment:

Shared Organizational Vision. As explored in Chapter 4, leaders are essential in shaping the vision and direction of the organization. This vision should be a clear and compelling picture of the organization's future, one that engages employees, provides meaning to their work, sets high standards of excellence, and connects current efforts to long-term goals. Importantly, this vision should not be developed in isolation but in collaboration with others.

Organizational Support. Empowerment is ineffective without the necessary resources to carry out the work. Resources can include decisionmaking authority, budget, technological tools, training, and other forms of support. When employees lack the appropriate resources to perform their tasks, it can lead to frustration, dissatisfaction, or even turnover.

Knowledge Sharing. In today's global economy, there is a strong emphasis on intellectual assets—knowledge that is embedded within the organization. As Betsy Anderson (2024) points out, seasoned employees hold a wealth of knowledge, from routine methods for achieving organizational goals to conceptual assets like customer data, research findings, patents, and systemic information such as policies and procedures. Promoting a culture of continuous learning and encouraging employees to share their knowledge and expertise is essential for organizational growth.

Rewards and Recognition. Empowerment often results in creative new products or services, and employees expect to be recognized for these contributions. Organizations have many ways to reward innovation, including cash bonuses, public recognition through internal or external awards, development opportunities, "facetime" with senior leaders, gifts or prizes, or promotions to manage new projects. Companies like Apple, Disney, Cisco, Unilever, Amazon, and American Airlines are known for their outstanding employee reward and recognition programs. For instance, Unilever invites its employees to evaluate their reward packages to gain insight into how staff perceive their benefits and to gather suggestions for enhancements, ensuring the rewards align with what employees truly value. Apple offers its employees stock options, discounts on products, and incentives for volunteering. Similarly, after one year of employment, Amazon covers 95% of tuition costs for courses teaching high-demand skills, even if those skills are unrelated to the company's operations.

Delegating responsibility—entrusting employees with key tasks—gives them the chance to grow and develop. It allows them to showcase their skills, builds self-confidence, and strengthens their commitment to the organization, making them feel valued and respected. Empowerment and delegation are gifts that, when embraced by the organization, foster loyalty, commitment, and improved work-life quality. This results in a happier, more engaged, and more productive workforce.

Lessons from the Trenches

Sidnice is employed by a national company that builds and manages single-story apartment homes. She works as a Human Resources Manager and is responsible for managing all aspects of the HR lifecycle. In one instance, she received a text message asking if they could terminate a long-term employee for allegedly threatening a customer. Sidnice recommended to the Vice President (VP) of Human Resources that the employee be suspended pending a thorough investigation. However, the VP reacted with a verbal outburst, accusing Sidnice of not taking the situation seriously enough.

Sidnice explained that the VP was receiving secondhand information since the incident had occurred in another state and was being reported by the Regional Manager. Despite Sidnice's advice, the VP proceeded to authorize the termination and instructed Sidnice to prepare the documentation. Sidnice refused to sign off on the termination because it did not align with proper HR procedures. She stated, "My role is not just to check boxes. I was hired to offer guidance, but they bypassed me and only sought my approval after the fact."

In an attempt to resolve the issue, Sidnice proposed a meeting with all involved parties to educate them on the proper termination process. The invitation was declined, and communication regarding the matter was cut off. Sidnice emphasized that, while she understood the gravity of the employee's misconduct, her stance was that suspension pending an investigation would have been the appropriate action. An investigation might still have supported the termination, but it would have ensured that proper documentation was in place in case of any legal action. Ultimately, the employee was suspended for five days, which aligned with Sidnice's original recommendation and validated her approach.

When reflecting on the VP's actions, Sidnice highlighted the following concerns:

- The VP's actions made her feel that there was a lack of trust. Despite working for the organization for two years and consistently receiving "Exceeded Expectations" ratings, she felt undermined and devalued in this situation.

- The VP's verbal outburst was unprofessional and demonstrated a lack of decorum. The unexpected behavior made Sidnice reluctant to continue sharing her opinions, fostering a culture of silence within the organization.

- Management failed to delegate the task appropriately and did not empower Sidnice to handle the situation as she saw fit. Instead, the VP took control of the process, excluding her from a role she was hired to fulfill.

Lessons from the Trenches

- **Lesson:** Trusting employees with responsibilities and empowering them to make decisions is a hallmark of strong leadership. Leaders who delegate effectively show confidence in their team's abilities.

- **Impact:** Empowered employees feel more engaged and are likely to take ownership of their work, leading to higher productivity and innovation.

- **Lesson:** When employees are given autonomy and trust, they often take greater ownership of their work and contribute more creatively.

- **Impact:** Leaders can learn to delegate more effectively, empowering their teams and fostering a culture of accountability and innovation.

For Reflection:

Leaders who delegate effectively demonstrate trust in their team's skills. These prompts are designed to help leaders reflect on how they can foster a culture that promotes and supports thoughtful delegation among their team members.

1. Do leaders within the organization consistently seek input from their team, and are their ideas actively considered in decisionmaking processes?

2. How can leaders create more opportunities for team members to highlight their strengths and take the lead on projects?

3. Are leaders genuinely receptive to different perspectives, even when they challenge their own instincts or views?

4. In what ways can leaders empower their teams to drive the organization's objectives forward?

5. How can leaders apply the Situational Leadership Model to promote delegation and empowerment across the organization?

CHAPTER 7 Decrease Subjectivity and Increase Objectivity

A leader's job is not to do the work for others, it's to help others figure out how to do it themselves, to get things done, and to succeed beyond what they thought possible.

~ Simon Sinek, Author

Some organizations view their employees as their most valuable asset. NASA, for instance, exemplifies this with its Human Capital mantra, "People First, Mission Always," emphasizing that when an organization takes care of its people, they, in turn, are well-equipped to achieve the mission at hand. A company's true success is often gauged by the effectiveness of its employees, which is commonly assessed through some form of performance evaluation.

Most organizations implement performance appraisal systems to assess how well employees meet their goals and objectives. According to Fred Lunenburg, a professor at Sam Houston State University, performance appraisal refers to the process by which supervisors evaluate the performance of their subordinates, typically on an annual or semiannual basis, to inform decisions on raises, promotions, or training needs (Lunenburg, 2012). However, performance reviews can also induce stress and anxiety for employees, affecting their overall well-being, job satisfaction, and productivity. The challenge for organizations lies in creating a performance management system that minimizes subjectivity and increases objectivity, ensuring employees feel their performance is assessed equitably.

As Dick Grote (1996) pointed out, a well-structured appraisal process can shift a company from a culture of effort to one that emphasizes results. Over time, performance appraisals have evolved, moving away from subjective measures toward more objective criteria, transitioning from abstract evaluations of personality to concrete assessments of performance (Kavanagh, 1971). While reducing subjectivity is important, it cannot be eliminated entirely. Many scholars argue that a balanced approach—incorporating both subjective and objective elements—depending on the nature of the job is essential. Michael Kavanagh (1971) suggests that relying solely on objective criteria can be misleading, and some roles may require more subjective, personalitybased evaluations. For instance, sales positions may include personality factors in performance reviews, as successful salespeople often possess outgoing personalities that help them connect with clients. However, their evaluations should also incorporate objective metrics, such as conversion rates and sales per quarter.

This chapter will explore various approaches to performance appraisals, common challenges in the evaluation process, and best practices for delivering and receiving feedback.

Approaches to Performance Management

A strong connection to an organization's mission is essential for fostering employee engagement. Employees tend to be more satisfied when they believe in their work and understand how it contributes to the organization's overall mission. Therefore, leaders must ensure that performance standards, goals, and objectives for employees are clearly aligned with the broader goals of the organization. Managers should regularly ask themselves, "Do my team members understand how their daily tasks contribute to achieving the organization's goals and strategies?" If the answer is yes, employees should be able to articulate that connection. If not, it may be necessary to revisit the performance metrics to improve alignment.

According to the *Modernized Performance Management Report* by McLean & Company (n.d.), traditional performance management systems are often ineffective, and organizations should adopt approaches tailored to their specific contexts. Traditional systems are typically characterized by unclear connections between expectations and organizational goals, annual reviews, infrequent feedback, and subjective ratings, which can leave employees feeling disengaged and dissatisfied. In contrast, some organizations have adopted a more agile approach, where expectations are flexible, goals are revisited monthly, feedback and coaching are continuous, and there are no performance ratings or annual reviews. McLean & Company advocates for a modern approach to performance management that includes clear performance standards and expectations, quarterly and annual goal reviews, more frequent feedback and coaching, and objective ratings, where appropriate, supplemented by employee selfassessments. By modernizing performance management systems, organizations can boost employee engagement and productivity.

Three Approaches to Performance Appraisals

If an organization chooses to adopt a modern performance management approach, leaders will need to determine the most suitable method for conducting quarterly and annual performance reviews. According to Lunenburg (2012), there are three main approaches to performance appraisals: judgment-based, absolute standards, and results-oriented. He defines these approaches as follows:

- **Judgment-Based**: Leaders utilize four primary mechanisms: graphic rating scales, ranking, paired comparisons, and forced distribution. The most commonly used tool in organizations is the graphic rating scale, often based on a scale of 1 to 5.

- **Absolute Standards**: Managers assess employee performance against a predefined standard rather than comparing employees to one another. Common methods in this category include checklists, essays, critical incidents, and behaviorally anchored rating scales.

- **Results-Oriented**: This approach focuses on evaluating quantitative and qualitative outcomes rather than assessing traits or on-the-job behaviors. Supervisors set performance goals, either independently or collaboratively, with employees, and employee performance is measured against those goals at the end of the evaluation period.

While each of these approaches has its own advantages and drawbacks, the results-oriented method provides a balance of both objective and subjective criteria. The emphasis should remain on objective or judgment-based metrics, while subjective considerations, such as on-thejob behaviors only, should be factored in based on the nature of the role.

Challenges to Performance Evaluations

Despite efforts to remain unbiased, personal perceptions and biases often affect the evaluation process. Managers, consciously or unconsciously, can be influenced by preconceived notions or interpersonal dynamics, leading to skewed assessments. Lunenburg (2012) highlights several common challenges leaders encounter during performance evaluations, including strictness or leniency tendencies, the halo effect, and a focus on recent events:

- **Strictness or Leniency Tendencies**: Strict evaluators tend to give lower ratings than deserved, while lenient evaluators assign higher ratings. Both tendencies misrepresent employee performance. Strict raters may harm motivation, while lenient raters may create a false sense of competency.

- **Halo Effect**: When a manager views an employee positively in one area, they may tend to rate them similarly across all categories. Conversely, a negative view in one area can lead to lower ratings in other aspects.

- **Recency of Events**: When managers base their evaluations primarily on recent performance and neglect the entire review period, it results in unbalanced assessments influenced by momentary factors.

To address these biases, managers should undergo unconscious bias training. Additional challenges with performance evaluations include:

Challenge	Solution
Inadequate Feedback: Annual reviews are too infrequent to be actionable or helpful.	Implement a modern approach with quarterly feedback to make evaluations timelier and more useful.
Misalignment with Organizational Goals: Performance standards are sometimes too narrow and miss broader objectives.	Align performance metrics with organizational strategies, ensuring goals cascade throughout the organization.
Lack of Employee Engagement: Traditional systems can feel topdown and exclude employee input.	Adopt a collaborative approach to performance standards, incorporating employee feedback and clarifying expectations.

Performance reviews are essential to effective organizational management, yet traditional methods frequently pose significant challenges. By recognizing these issues and implementing targeted solutions, organizations can create a more streamlined, fair, and comprehensive performance management system that aligns with both individual and organizational goals.

Performance Evaluations Procedures

Some supervisors may feel uneasy about conducting performance discussions with employees, especially when corrective actions are necessary. However, these conversations can be one of the most effective tools for motivating a team. Herman Aguinis and colleagues observed that traditional performance appraisals often focus on identifying and addressing gaps in employees' performance, knowledge, and skills (Aguinis et al., 2012).

Some experts, like Thomas Alvarez (1996), argue that performance reviews should be conducted at least four times a year rather than annually, providing more opportunities to address and correct behaviors as they arise. Performance issues should not be broached for the first time during formal reviews; instead, supervisors should address concerns immediately when they surface. Failing to do so sends a message that the problematic behavior or performance is acceptable.

Since performance discussions can sometimes be uncomfortable, some supervisors avoid them altogether. To address this, an alternative approach has been suggested—one that emphasizes an employee's strengths rather than focusing on deficiencies. This appreciative approach can be more motivating for some employees.

For performance evaluations to be effective, Chris Obisi (2011) outlined several key steps:

1. **Establish performance standards**: These should include clear, measurable, and time-bound objectives. Depending on the role, subjective elements like communication and teamwork can also be included. Involving the employee in defining these standards increases their commitment and buy-in.

2. **Communicate the standards clearly**: Both the supervisor and employee need a shared understanding of the performance expectations to ensure clarity on how to meet or exceed them.

3. **Measure performance continuously**: Throughout the year, supervisors should evaluate performance while avoiding biases such as strictness, leniency, the halo effect, and recency. Using clear rating mechanisms like scales ensures transparency in the process.

4. **Discuss the appraisal with the employee**: Regular feedback fosters open communication.

5. **Reward or correct performance when necessary**: Timely recognition or corrective action helps reinforce or guide employee behavior.

Giving and Receiving Feedback

Delivering both positive and constructive feedback is a key element in the employee appraisal process. A study by Price Waterhouse Coopers (PwC) found that "75% of employees who receive feedback consider it highly valuable to their work. Additionally, 45% of respondents appreciate feedback from peers and customers, yet fewer than 30% actually receive it" (PwC, 2011). Millennials, in particular, view regular feedback as crucial for their career growth and as a factor in deciding whether to stay with an organization.

For instance, employees may feel dissatisfied for several reasons, such as:

- A lack of guidance on how to improve performance and grow in their roles.

- Perceived unfairness in how performance reviews are conducted or how ratings are assigned.

- Unclear expectations regarding the level of effort required to achieve a certain rating.

- A disconnect between performance ratings and compensation, rewards, or recognition.

Simply giving feedback is not enough; positive and constructive feedback needs to be part of a two-way conversation. Gallup reports that only 26% of employees strongly agree that the feedback they receive helps them improve (Wigert & Dvorak, 2019). This is often because feedback sessions are one-sided, with little opportunity for employee input. Traditional performance reviews typically involve a manager outlining how an employee performed against set standards over a specific period. However, performance discussions are most effective when they are conversational and involve self-assessment from the employee. While managers should still offer constructive feedback, they should first allow employees to evaluate their own performance and then build on that by highlighting successes and areas for improvement that the employee may not have recognized.

The discussion should begin with the employee's self-assessment and conclude with a conversation about career aspirations and future goals.

To help employees prepare for the review, here are some questions you can provide beforehand for their self-assessment:

1. What accomplishments are you most proud of from the last performance cycle?

2. What, if anything, would you have done differently?

3. Which specific initiative or project you would like to work on?

4. How do you think you can contribute to the organization's goals?

5. How can I best support you in the upcoming performance cycle?

6. What improvements do you think we could make in our team or department?

For career development discussions during the appraisal, consider asking these questions:

1. What are your long-term career goals?

2. What skills would you like to develop?

3. What strengths do you feel you could build on?

4. What is one behavior you would like to improve or develop?

5. What, if any, obstacles may be holding you back?

6. What role do you see yourself transitioning too next?

The most important part of any performance conversation is outlining a clear path forward—identifying opportunities for employees to grow and develop. Asking where they envision themselves communicates that you care about their success, and then asking how you can best support them demonstrates that you are open to making the changes necessary to help them thrive.

Holding Employee Accountable

At times, an employee's behavior or performance may be so problematic that corrective action is necessary. Leaders need to understand their responsibility in managing both misconduct and performance issues.

Supervisors must be familiar with the organization's Human Resources policies, rules, and procedures that govern employee conduct and ensure these are communicated and applied consistently across teams. When rules are applied fairly and impartially, employees are more engaged, and decisions are easier to defend in case of legal challenges. In contrast, inconsistent application can lead to perceptions of favoritism within the workplace. Leaders should aim for transparency and consistency in their decision-making and the implementation of procedures.

When leaders establish clear, objective performance standards tied to specific, time-bound goals, it becomes the employee's responsibility to meet those targets. Success should be rewarded, while failure may lead to actions such as performance improvement plans or, in some cases, termination. Performance reviews are intended to give employees feedback and the opportunity to meet or exceed expectations. If performance falls short, then a specific period—typically of 30 to 90 days—should be given to allow for improvement. If leaders are uncertain about how to address the situation, they should consult Human Resources for guidance to ensure that their actions align with the organization's policies and procedures.

Lessons from the Trenches

I led a team of employee development specialists, overseeing learning and development (L&D), organizational development (OD), performance management, and awards. While the L&D and OD functions were well integrated, the performance management and awards functions operated in silos. My team consisted of individuals with diverse experience levels, ranging from early career to more senior positions, including contractors, most of whom had more than 20 years of experience.

Upon taking on this role, I encountered several leadership challenges and a stagnant work environment. Issues included a lack of accountability, underperformance in delivering results, unclear roles and responsibilities, and an absence of a cohesive vision for the team. Additionally, there were interpersonal dynamics within the team that hindered progress, such as negative attitudes and apathy. Adding complexity to the situation, I had previously worked alongside the team as a peer, and now, in a supervisory role, some tension arose.

To foster team cohesion, I instituted bi-weekly meetings to provide updates, listen to concerns, and encourage open dialogue. I introduced a visual career board to share my background, values, and expectations and had each team member create their own graphic representing their career, family, and values. This exercise helped build empathy among the team, broke down barriers, and clarified my supervisory role, authority, and responsibilities.

Some team members struggled with performance, with one employee consistently missing key milestones and submitting low-quality work that required significant revisions. For those facing challenges, I held weekly check-ins to clarify expectations, prioritize tasks, and support their goal achievement. These sessions also allowed for personal engagement and status updates on upcoming deliverables. I took the time to understand each team member's career aspirations, allocated funding for professional development, and provided stretch assignments to enhance their visibility and skills within the organization.

For the employee who was not meeting performance standards, I collaborated with HR to implement a performance improvement plan. Unfortunately, despite the support provided, the employee chose to retire rather than improve their performance. While the aim is always to help employees succeed, improvement requires a willingness to engage and take responsibility.

Ultimately, two of the three struggling employees transformed their performance, meeting and even exceeding expectations. Their significant progress earned them agency honor awards for the first time in their careers. My goal was to re-engage every team member and support them in achieving both personal and organizational objectives. I raised performance standards, ensuring both praise and constructive feedback were delivered fairly and without bias. I believe that fairness fosters a culture of responsibility and trust, where employees feel valued and motivated to rise to the expectations set for them.

Lessons from the Trenches

- **Lesson:** Effective leaders hold themselves and others accountable. They ensure that praise and constructive feedback are delivered fairly, without bias.

- **Impact:** This fairness builds a culture of responsibility and trust, where employees feel that they are treated equitably.

For Reflection:

Performance management plays a vital role in shaping organizational culture and driving job performance, productivity, and employee wellbeing. The following reflective questions can help evaluate the effectiveness of the organization's performance management system:

1. How does the organization ensure alignment between individual performance goals and broader company objectives?

2. What measures can be implemented to minimize personal biases in appraisals and promote fairness and objectivity?

3. What approaches can leaders take to address underperformance, fostering improvement while maintaining accountability?

4. How do you engage employees in their own performance development and career progression?

5. What are the primary challenges leaders face during performance appraisals, and how are they resolved?

6. What techniques do you use to ensure performance reviews focus not just on past achievements but also on future growth potential?

CHAPTER 8 Honest and Sincere Appreciation

Next to physical survival, the greatest need of a human being is psychological survival: to be understood, to be affirmed, to be validated, to be appreciated.

~ Stephen Covey, Author

To enhance employee morale, job satisfaction, and overall productivity, leaders should prioritize providing honest and sincere appreciation in the workplace. In an article in *Harvard Business Review*, Mike Robbins highlighted the distinction between recognition and appreciation (Robbins, 2019). He explained that while recognition is feedback tied to results or performance, appreciation acknowledges an individual's inherent value. As Stephen Covey emphasized, appreciation is a fundamental human need and must be present in the workplace.

According to Globalforce (2012), having a recognition program is not enough; it needs to be strategically aligned with the organization's core values and objectives. This adds purpose to employees' work by helping them understand how their contributions drive organizational success. Their 2012 Employee Recognition Survey found that employees at companies with strategic recognition programs are 21.5% more empowered to contribute to organizational objectives than those at companies without such programs (Globalforce, 2012). Additionally, 37% of companies with strategic recognition reported higher levels of employee engagement compared to 25% of companies without these programs (Globalforce, 2012).

In a 2003 National Recognition Survey by WorldatWork and the National Association for Employee Recognition (NAER), 87% of respondents indicated they had some form of employee recognition program, and 40% were expanding these initiatives (Daniel & Metcalf, 2005).

When employees feel appreciated and acknowledged, organizations often see higher employee engagement, reduced turnover, and improved customer satisfaction (Robbins, 2019). Employees not only feel their efforts are valued, but they also find greater meaning in their work.

In this chapter, we will delve into different forms of appreciation and examine the advantages and challenges of establishing appreciation practices in the workplace.

Forms of Appreciation

Employee compensation, including wages, salaries, bonuses, commissions, incentives, merit pay, and stock options, directly reflects their job performance and plays a vital role in motivating them (Akafo

& Boateng, 2015). One way to transform an employee's "paycheck into purpose" is to create a well-rounded appreciation and recognition program that offers both financial and non-financial rewards, helping employees feel more purposeful and connected to their work.

Dr. Gary Chapman, the bestselling author of *The 5 Love Languages* series, comes from a background in marriage counseling. During one counseling session, a supervisor mentioned to him that the five love languages could be relevant not only to marriages but also to workplace relationships, referring to them as "appreciation languages." Intrigued by this idea, Dr. Chapman partnered with psychologist Dr. Paul White, who had experience in both counseling and business, to explore whether the five love languages could effectively be applied in the workplace, and they found that they did.

For over two decades, they have helped various organizations, including businesses, schools, government agencies, and nonprofits, to:

- Boost staff morale and foster positive work environments.
- Teach leaders how to show authentic, personalized appreciation to team members.
- Minimize negativity, sarcasm, and cynicism in toxic work cultures.
- Create a supportive atmosphere by addressing common barriers to workplace recognition.

Together, Drs. Chapman and White co-authored *The 5 Languages of Appreciation in the Workplace*. Their research found that 79% of employees who leave their jobs cite a lack of appreciation as a major factor, while 65% of North American employees reported not receiving any recognition at work in the past year (Chapman & White, 2019). The five appreciation languages are:

1. **Words of Affirmation** – Using positive, specific language, either spoken or written, to express appreciation. This could be one-on-one praise, recognition in front of others, or even a written note, but it should always highlight specific actions, not just a general thank you.

2. **Quality Time** – Giving someone undivided attention through meaningful interactions. Whether it is working alongside them, holding brief meetings, engaging in decision-making discussions, or simply chatting during the day, this form of appreciation emphasizes shared experiences and personal connection.

3. **Acts of Service** – Providing help and support, regardless of job role, when someone needs assistance. Key principles include asking if help is needed, offering voluntary and cheerful assistance, following the other person's preferences, and ensuring the task is completed with care.

4. **Tangible Gifts** – Offering a physical token of appreciation that aligns with the recipient's interests, values, or hobbies. While some organizations recognize employees with tangible gifts, others do not. The key is focusing on something that resonates personally with the individual. Sometimes, organizational policies restrict gift-giving, especially when it comes to costly items. In

such situations, simple gestures like taking an employee to lunch or hosting an office potluck are often the most common form of appreciation.

5. **Physical Touch** – This form of appreciation is seldom an employee's primary appreciation language in the workplace. It has the potential to either uplift or cause discomfort. Drs. Chapman and White noted that appropriate gestures such as celebratory high-fives, fist bumps, pats on the back, and handshakes can be effective when used thoughtfully and spontaneously. Other forms of unwanted physical touch can lead to sexual harassment complaints in the workplace.

These five languages of appreciation offer a wide spectrum of ways to acknowledge employees and ensure they feel valued. It is essential to recognize that if appreciation is not expressed in an individual's preferred language, the gesture may not have the intended impact. Leaders should take the time to understand their team members' preferred methods of appreciation and act accordingly.

Benefits of Appreciation Programs

In a white paper from the Society for Human Resource Management (SHRM), the authors observed that organizations where employees genuinely enjoy working are those that consistently recognize their staff (Daniel & Metcalf, 2005). These companies do not just offer verbal praise but also demonstrate appreciation through concrete actions like incentives, recognition, and rewards. As a result, organizations that foster a culture of appreciation enjoy numerous benefits, such as a strengthened organizational culture, increased performance and productivity, higher employee retention, improved morale, and enhanced collaboration (Ramya & Vanithamani, 2023).

- **Enhanced Organizational Culture** – When appreciation is central to the workplace, employees feel more valued, motivated, and engaged.

- **Increased Performance and Productivity** – Recognized employees are more likely to put in discretionary effort, leading to greater commitment and higher productivity.

- **Higher Retention Rates** – Companies that prioritize employee recognition tend to have lower turnover rates, as employees feel more valued.

- **Boosted Employee Morale** – Acknowledging employees for their contributions fosters a sense of accomplishment and purpose, improving overall happiness and well-being at work.

- **Improved Teamwork and Collaboration** – Recognition flows in all directions—top-down, bottom-up, and laterally. In a culture where recognition is valued, employees feel more motivated and are encouraged to acknowledge the contributions of their peers. This creates a positive cycle of recognition, leading to better teamwork, clearer communication, and greater synergy within teams.

Challenges with Appreciation Programs

Experts widely agree that recognition and appreciation in the workplace are beneficial, with organizations often seeing improved employee engagement, reduced turnover, and higher customer satisfaction rates (Robbins, 2019). However, implementing these programs can be complex. Ramya & Vanithamani (2023) identified several challenges in fostering a culture of appreciation, including:

- **Lack of Personalization**: Generic approaches may fail to address the specific needs and context of each organization.

- **Industry-Specific Limitations**: Different sectors, such as the government, have unique rules and constraints that can restrict the types of rewards that can be given, including monetary awards or gifts.

- **Perceived Unfairness**: If the criteria and processes for recognition are unclear, employees may feel that favoritism or inequity is at play.

- **Over-Reliance on Monetary Rewards**: While financial incentives are important, an overemphasis on them can overshadow non-monetary recognition like verbal praise, work flexibility, or professional growth opportunities.

- **Sustainability Issues**: Programs must be continuously monitored and updated to remain effective over time rather than fading away after initial enthusiasm.

Components of an Effective Recognition and Appreciation Program

Teresa A. Daniel, J.D., and Gary S. Metcalf, Ph.D., highlight key elements necessary for the success of recognition and appreciation programs. These include management buy-in, alignment with organizational goals, valuing employees, fairness, simplicity, and regular evaluation (Daniel & Metcalf, 2005). A critical aspect of any recognition program is active managerial involvement, as managers are responsible for identifying employees whose performance merits recognition.

Recognition should be tied directly to organizational goals, helping employees understand how their work contributes to the overall success of the company, thereby adding purpose and meaning to their efforts. Additionally, recognition must be tailored to what the individual employee values most. One tool for determining this is the Motivating by Appreciation (MBA) Inventory, developed by Drs. Gary Chapman and Paul White help leaders understand and deliver recognition in a way that resonates with each employee.

To ensure fairness, organizations should create transparent, objective criteria for recognition, sharing these guidelines with all employees to make the process clear. It's also important to keep recognition programs simple, relevant, and timely—employees are more likely to engage in programs that are straightforward and provide immediate recognition rather than those that are bogged down by complex, time-consuming processes.

A practical approach to recognizing contributions is the E.A.R. formula: **Evaluation + Action = Results**.

- **Evaluation**: Regularly monitor and assess employee performance against defined criteria.

- **Action**: Take timely steps to reward performance and behavior that aligns with organizational objectives and values.

- **Results**: Organizations that emphasize recognition tend to experience higher productivity and profitability.

The primary goal of any appreciation or recognition program is to inspire individuals to sustain high levels of performance or positive behavior (Ho & Nguyen, 2021). To ensure these programs are effective, organizations should regularly, or at least annually, assess their impact. This can be done by gathering employee feedback through climate surveys or informal conversations during performance reviews to gauge whether employees feel acknowledged and appreciated. If the program is falling short of its goals, the organization should reassess and make the necessary changes to ensure it achieves its intended outcomes.

Lessons from the Trenches

Kathy spent four decades serving in the federal government, having begun her career straight out of high school. Given several career paths, Kathy chose to focus on learning and development, dedicating herself to supporting the growth and development of employees. When she started, she did not have a disability, but later in life, she was diagnosed with Multiple Sclerosis (MS). Despite this, Kathy became a passionate advocate for Diversity, Equity, Inclusion, and Accessibility (DEIA), leading the Disability Awareness and Advisory Group (DAAG) for more than a decade. She also shared her expertise as a panelist at the Accessibility Conference: Promoting Disability Inclusion in the Workplace, where she encouraged individuals with disabilities to seek personal and professional growth through the support of managers and advisory groups. At the conference, she expressed her hopes for a future where disabled individuals face no barriers and can reach their full potential in the workplace. Her lifelong commitment to accessibility and inclusion has positively impacted underrepresented groups within her organization.

Despite her significant contributions, Kathy had not previously received formal recognition for her efforts within the disability community. However, after her supervisor attended a session on the 5 Languages of Appreciation, everything changed. She learned that Kathy's primary appreciation style was Words of Affirmation and nominated her for two prestigious awards: the Agency Honor Award for Diversity, Equity, Inclusion, and Accessibility Medal and the Employee of the Year award from *Careers & the Disabled Magazine*. Kathy won both awards and was recognized at the agency's Annual Honor Award ceremony with the DEIA Medal, and her story was featured in both the *Careers & the Disabled Magazine* and an internal newsletter.

For Kathy, this recognition marked the first time in her 40-year career that she truly felt seen, heard, and valued within the organization. She was deeply honored by the acknowledgment of her contributions on both an agency and national level. This validation not only boosted her performance but also inspired her to be more innovative and proactive in improving the programs she manages. Kathy now feels an even greater sense of purpose and commitment to her work.

Lessons from the Trenches

- **Lesson**: Every employee—from the board room to the mail room—values recognition for their hard work and contributions. Leaders and organizations alike can benefit from regularly acknowledging and celebrating employee achievements.

- **Impact**: Regular recognition boosts morale, increases job satisfaction, and motivates employees to continually strive for and maintain higher levels of performance and greater results.

For Reflection:

Employee recognition programs can play a crucial role in boosting morale, enhancing job satisfaction, and motivating employees to sustain higher levels of performance. The following reflective questions can help assess the structure and impact of current recognition programs:

1. Does the organization's culture actively support a recognition program? What are the program's purpose criteria, and who is responsible for managing it?

2. Is the program aligned with the organization's strategic goals and objectives?

3. What ceremonies or rituals are associated with the program? Do employees find them meaningful and valuable?

4. Are managers equipped and trained in different recognition methods to use the program effectively?

5. How frequently is the program reviewed for effectiveness, and does it positively influence employee motivation and performance?

CHAPTER 9 The Career Architect

I think one of the keys to leadership is recognizing that

everyone has gifts and talents.

A good leader will learn how to harness those gifts

towards the same goal.

~ Ben Carson, Former U.S. Secretary of Housing and Urban

Development

Today's workforce, particularly early career employees, is more focused on career growth than ever before. Gallup (2021) highlighted how COVID-19 significantly impacted the U.S. economy, causing frequent shifts in workforce participation as people entered and left jobs. The cost of replacing an employee is estimated to be about 1.5 times the salary of the vacated position (Merchant, 2010). Historically, from the 1950s through the 1970s, employees demonstrated strong loyalty to their organizations. However, as downsizing became more common, this loyalty diminished, fundamentally altering the employee-employer contract (Van Velsor et al., 2010). Gone are the days when employees stayed with a company for their entire career and retired from it. Now, employees take ownership of their careers, often choosing employers that prioritize their personal development and growth. This shift has led organizations to focus on upskilling, whether by teaching new skills or enhancing existing ones (Gallup, 2021). According to Gallup (2021), 65% of workers consider upskilling a critical factor in accepting job offers, and 59% of current employees are eager to improve their skills to advance in their careers. By investing in career development, organizations can maintain their capabilities and better prepare for future challenges.

Employee development brings numerous benefits. For employees, it may lead to salary increases, career advancement, and greater job satisfaction (Gallup, 2021). Prospective employees are drawn to employers who are willing to invest in their long-term growth (Gurchiek, 2022). For employers, offering development opportunities helps attract and retain a skilled workforce while boosting employee engagement (Gallup, 2021). Gurchiek (2022) also suggests that early-career employees, in particular, expect robust development programs, which is a key factor influencing their choice of employer. Gallup's (2021) research found that 61% of workers stay with their employers because of strong development opportunities.

This chapter will explore the significance of career development in attracting, nurturing, and retaining talent while providing practical tools for leaders to effectively manage their teams.

Maintaining a Competitive Advantage

In traditional hierarchical and bureaucratic organizations, career development was often seen as a linear progression up the corporate ladder. Employees were expected to work diligently, remain loyal, and gain experience over time, with the eventual reward of advancing to higher positions. Early career employees were typically viewed as inexperienced and required to "pay their dues" by gaining hands-on experience before they could significantly contribute to the organization's goals and objectives.

In contrast, 21st-century employees have redefined what a career looks like and how to accelerate their advancement. Robert Lent & Steven Brown (2013) described a career as a series of jobs held over one's lifetime, and research indicates that the average person will hold approximately 12 jobs throughout their career (Kurtuy, 2024). This trend makes it unlikely that new hires will stay with an organization until retirement, which drives up the cost of replacing employees. As a result, companies focus on attracting top talent and offering incentives to retain them. So, what do employees expect? Early-career professionals seek competitive salaries as they begin their careers, but more importantly, they look for growth opportunities such as mentorship, learning experiences, and a supportive company culture.

Kathy Gurchiek (2024) highlighted findings from a survey conducted by SHRM and Handshake, which gathered responses from 2,122 U.S. students and recent graduates, as well as 1,180 Human Resources (HR) professionals involved in hiring emerging talent. The survey found that most early career hires possess skills such as adaptability, eagerness to learn, and strong communication abilities. However, employers seek additional qualities like reliability, critical thinking, and effective time management. The survey revealed that 69% of early career hires prioritize job security when evaluating potential employers, while 66% place high value on professional development opportunities.

Training and career development remain essential for both early career and seasoned employees. Nearly one-third (32%) of recent graduates expect to stay in their current jobs for four or more years (Gurchiek,

2024). However, twice as many (65%) would stay for more than four years if their employer offered growth opportunities within the organization (Gurchiek, 2024).

Providing career development opportunities offers numerous benefits. Organizations that prioritize career development are often seen as "Employers of Choice," attracting individuals not only for personal gain but also for the chance to contribute to the organization's mission. Employees benefit from increased salaries, career progression, and enhanced job satisfaction (Gallup, 2021). Workers are drawn to employers that invest in their long-term success and professional growth (Gurchiek, 2022). Employers also benefit by attracting and retaining a highly skilled workforce while increasing employee engagement (Gallup, 2021). Stuart Conger (2002) noted that cultivating a culture of career development can improve productivity, competitiveness, and succession planning, helping organizations maintain their competitive advantage in the marketplace.

Managing Talent

Effectively managing the workforce requires a deliberate approach, which includes creating a comprehensive talent management strategy (TMS). This strategy should be formulated at the organization's highest levels and must feature a process for identifying key roles and high-potential employees, including a gap analysis (Carbery & Cross, 2017). Additionally, the strategy should include a well-structured implementation plan with evaluation criteria to measure its success (Carbery & Cross, 2017). The ability to attract and retain top talent is crucial to an organization's long-term sustainability and competitiveness in the ongoing

"global talent war."

Faria Rabbi and fellow researchers (2015) contend that talent is the only resource capable of providing a sustainable competitive edge for many organizations. However, there are numerous challenges in talent management, such as attracting a highly skilled workforce, fostering a culture of open knowledge-sharing despite concerns that withholding knowledge offers individual advantages, and navigating cultural barriers (Rabbi et al., 2015).

| DEVELOP A STRATEGY | ATTRACT & RETAIN | MOTIVATE & DEVELOP | DEPLOY & MANAGE | CONNECT & ENABLE | TRANSFORM & SUSTAIN |

In the book *Agile Career Development*, Mary Ann Bopp and fellow researchers (2009) outline six key dimensions of talent management:

1. **Develop a Strategy** – Create a forward-thinking, long-term plan for attracting, developing, and utilizing talent. Organizations must anticipate what knowledge, skills, and abilities will be essential in the future, as the skills needed today may not suffice tomorrow. Thus, it is crucial to consider broader future needs. When defining both current and future requirements, ask:

- What projects, programs, and challenges are on the horizon for the organization in the next five years? How will the nature of the work evolve?

- What specific competencies (knowledge, skills, and abilities) will be necessary to meet these challenges?

- Are these competencies already present within the organization?

- Are there gaps in these competencies, and what recruitment strategies will help bridge them?

2. **Attract and Retain Talent** – Focus on sourcing, recruiting, and keeping the right talent to meet organizational goals. To effectively attract new talent and retain high-potential employees, the organization must offer a compelling vision for the future and provide professional development opportunities that foster growth. Early career employees, in particular, look for benefits like tuition assistance and skill development programs.

3. **Motivate and Develop Talent** – Ensure that employees' skills align with the organization's business goals. Employees want to feel that their day-to-day work contributes meaningfully to an organization's mission. One way to accomplish this is by making sure that employee performance plans are tied to the organization's strategy and include discussions on development.

4. **Deploy and Manage Talent** – Optimize the allocation of resources by matching employees' skills and experience to organizational needs. Some organizations have critical functions

where only a few personnel are available. It is important to build internal bench strength by encouraging employees to gain experience across departments to fill gaps.

5. **Connect and Enable Talent** – Providing employees with the tools and resources they need to stay connected is vital in today's hybrid global workforce. Foster collaboration, knowledge sharing, and effective teamwork across the organization.

6. **Transform and Sustain** – Organizations must balance transformation initiatives with maintaining ongoing business activities. Drive sustainable change while ensuring the continuity of daily operations.

By systematically attracting, developing, motivating, and managing talent, an organization can maintain its competitive edge in the market (Hadijah, 2023).

Barriers to Career Development

Human Resources (HR) is frequently responsible for implementing development initiatives within organizations. However, HR departments are often underfunded and understaffed, which can leave them inadequately prepared to deliver strategic training and development programs effectively.

Human resource development (HRD) is closely tied to an organization's culture. It promotes long-term learning for individuals, teams, and the organization as a whole (Plakhotnik, 2014). On an individual level, an employee must not only acquire new knowledge and skills but also enhance cognitive abilities to interpret personal experiences, which shape attitudes and values (Plakhotnik, 2014). On the other hand, organizational learning focuses on recognizing emerging trends, market shifts, and innovations that could reshape industries, prompting the organization to adapt accordingly (Canton, 2015; Plakhotnik, 2014). Maria Plakhotnik (2014) argues that "learning organizations have ingrained a continuous and enhanced capacity to learn, adapt, and change into their culture" (p. 43). This is supported by organizational values, policies, procedures, and systems that encourage employee learning. The goal is to develop highly skilled individuals who are capable of critical thinking and making informed decisions (Plakhotnik, 2014).

For organizations to remain competitive in the modern era, strategic investment in HRD is essential. Martin McCracken and Mary Wallace (2000) define strategic HRD as "a proactive, system-wide intervention linked to strategic planning and cultural change" rather than merely a reactive measure to address immediate issues, such as learning new processes or procedures. To be effective, strategic HRD must align with the organization's vision, mission, and objectives, using HRD as a lever to drive business strategy (McCracken & Wallace, 2000). While HRD professionals or Chief Learning Officers may manage these efforts, senior leadership must champion the HRD strategy. Managers also play a pivotal role in aligning organizational and HRD strategies.

Furthermore, it's not enough to simply implement HRD programs— organizations must regularly evaluate their return on investment and adjust these programs based on feedback.

Becoming a Learning Organization

Investing in employee training reflects an organization's commitment to employee development and serves as a strong indicator of its organizational culture. When budgets are constrained, supporting functions such as Learning and Development (L&D) are often among the first to face cuts, as they can be expensive, and the return on investment (ROI) can be difficult to quantify. To navigate these financial challenges, organizations should reassess their L&D initiatives, prioritizing costeffective programs that yield substantial ROI, like on-the-job training through stretch assignments and job rotations.

Establishing an active learning culture is essential to fostering employee growth. This involves promoting curiosity, encouraging feedback and self-reflection, and creating an environment where exploration and experimentation are integral to learning (Collin et al., 2012). As Peter Senge (2014) notes, experimentation is inseparable from learning.

According to Ngesu Lewis and colleagues (2008), several factors contribute to creating a learning organization:

1. Leaders who model risk-taking and innovation.

2. Empowering employees with decentralized decision-making.

3. Maintaining skill inventories to share knowledge effectively.

4. Incentives and structures that encourage employee-led initiatives.

5. Weighing the long-term impact of decisions on colleagues and the organization.

6. Frequent cross-training opportunities.

7. Learning from practical experience.

8. Fostering a culture of feedback and constructive dialogue.

In addition, a development-focused culture is characterized by trust, openness, collaboration, risk-taking, and alignment between systems and messaging (Wickramaratne, 2013). In a true learning organization, every employee is expected to learn from their experiences and apply that knowledge to enhance their work and contribute to the organization's success.

However, there are notable barriers to becoming a learning organization (Abdullah, 2009). These include:

1. A shortage of skilled Human Resource Development professionals capable of conducting effective needs analyses and evaluations.

2. The challenge of attracting and retaining talent amid a competitive job market.

3. Communication difficulties faced by trainers in diverse or crosscultural environments.

4. Resistance to change from seasoned employees, particularly with regard to technological advancements, can sometimes be perceived as a poor investment.

5. Employee skepticism toward training leads to disengagement and reduced organizational performance.

Despite these challenges, organizations that prioritize learning and development see numerous benefits, including improved job satisfaction, reduced turnover, higher productivity, increased profitability, the development of leadership at all levels, and enhanced adaptability across the company (Andreev, 2012).

Facilitating a Learning Organization

As a global research organization, the Center for Creative Leadership (CCL) is a top leadership development provider. The CCL developed a research-based method of organizational learning called the 70-20-10 rule.

This approach suggests that individuals learn best when there are a variety of learning mediums available to them, including formal training, developmental relationships (e.g., coaching and mentoring), and on-thejob experiences. This approach emphasizes the pivotal role of challenging assignments in developing and retaining talent and the power of on-thejob experience in learning retention.

The 70-20-10 rule states:

- 70% of training should take place while on the job,

- 20% should be conducted informally through mentoring, and •

    10% should be conducted formally through training sessions.

70% On-the-Job Experience	20% Informal Learning	10% Formal Learning
Hands-on experience	Coaching	Academic programs
Job shadowing	Collaboration and networking opportunities	Cohort programs
Short- and long-term details and job rotations		Conferences
	Communities of Practice	Self-study
Special projects and stretch assignments	Mentoring	Structured learning
		Webinars
		Workshops

Employees are looking for more than traditional classroom or formal training but diverse developmental experiences (Gurchiek, 2022), including a personalized development plan with short and long-term goals to help advance their careers rather than being solely focused on their current jobs. Kate Rockwood (2022) stated that organizations are moving away from expensive multiday, offsite training events toward more focused micro-learning opportunities or stretch assignments. Early career and seasoned employees alike expect their supervisors to provide regular check-ins on their progress and provide feedback on their strengths and challenges (Gurchiek, 2022). In addition, they seek professional coaches, mentors, and opportunities to practice newly learned skills (Gurchiek, 2022). Regardless of the development opportunity—a training program, a stretch assignment, or a coaching or mentoring relationship—these developmental experiences will be richer if they contain an initial assessment, a challenge, and support (Van Velsor et al., 2010).

Individual Development Plan

Individual Development Plans (IDPs) are utilized for both new hires and seasoned employees. They offer new employees the opportunity to continue building their knowledge, skills, and abilities in a specific area while helping experienced employees stay updated on the latest advancements in their field (Greenan, 2016). High-performing individuals tend to set ambitious goals and are strongly committed to achieving them (Greenan, 2016).

IDPs differ from Performance Improvement Plans (PIPs). While an IDP focuses on helping employees with their career and personal development, enabling them to achieve both short- and long-term career goals, PIPs are aimed at addressing job performance issues and improving specific areas where an employee may be underperforming.

IDP Goals:

- Enhance current job performance and learn new skills.

- Increase engagement, job satisfaction, and the challenge within one's role.

- Gain the knowledge, skills, and abilities required to meet career and personal aspirations that align with the organization's objectives.

An IDP is NOT:

- A performance evaluation.

- A Performance Improvement Plan.

- A formal contract between an employee and their supervisor.

- A method to clarify or revise a job description.

- A guarantee of promotion upon the completion of development objectives.

- A tool for resolving conflicts between a manager and an employee.

- A one-time activity.

Merchant (2010) emphasizes that action plans must be clearly defined, detailing the concrete steps required for an employee's career advancement. These plans should be realistic and measurable to allow both the employee and the organization to assess progress. They should include specific, attainable development objectives, as well as the necessary resources to support these goals. Additionally, the plan must remain flexible to allow employees to reassess their individual needs and ambitions as their careers evolve.

Roles and Responsibilities in Career Development

In the book *Agile Career Development*, Mary Ann Bopp and colleagues (2009) explained that employees are driven by roles that challenge them and offer opportunities for growth and learning. Conversely, they become demotivated in jobs that are repetitive or offer no room for advancement. A 2023 survey by INTOO, a career development and outplacement firm, revealed some key insights: 54% of employees feel they are on their own when it comes to career development guidance; 44% of Gen Z and 25% of all employees—are likely to resign within the next six months due to a lack of career support from their company; and 6% of employees report that their supervisors do not know how to help them advance their careers (INTOO, 2023).

Career development serves to align individual goals with organizational objectives, ensuring employees build long-term capabilities that benefit both their careers and the company's strategic plans (Bopp et al., 2009).

In their article, *The New Protean Career Contract*, Douglas Hall & Jonathan Moss (1998) described the roles and responsibilities of both employees and supervisors:

Employee Responsibilities:

- Take ownership of their development and initiate the IDP process.
- Identify the knowledge, skills, and abilities required for their current role.
- Explore potential learning opportunities.
- Seek guidance from a career counselor or mentor to draft the IDP and prepare for discussions with their supervisor.
- Discuss the IDP with their supervisor and secure agreement on learning opportunities.
- Once proficient in their current role, begin setting objectives for higher-level tasks.

Supervisor Responsibilities:

- Identify the knowledge, skills, and abilities needed for the employee's current job.

- Provide constructive feedback.

- Serve as a coach, offering guidance on developmental activities to achieve the employee's IDP goals.

- Define realistic development activities that align with organizational priorities and resources and match employees to assignments that emphasize developmental benefits.

- Encourage learning through relationships, such as coaching and mentorship.

At a minimum, supervisors should meet with employees annually to assess the skills needed to meet business goals, discuss career aspirations, and create an individual development plan that balances both the employee's growth and the organization's objectives (Bopp et al., 2009).

Lessons from the Trenches

A supervisor's role as a *Career Navigator* involves guiding employees in achieving their professional goals while aligning developmental activities with organizational needs. Nola shared her winding career path, highlighting those who supported and guided her along the way.

In high school, Nola dreamed of going away to college and majoring in business, but when her mother became ill, she made the difficult decision to stay home, care for her, and enter the workforce instead. She started working in a counseling office at Cuyahoga Community College (TriC), where she was presented with an opportunity to work for a federal contractor as a file clerk.

Following three years as a contractor, a Division Chief presented Nola with an opportunity to join the civil service as a secretary, inspiring her to return to school and continue her education. After six years in the secretarial role, Nola applied for a position in Human Resources. With the support of LeRoy, the hiring manager, who helped her recognize her transferable skills, she successfully transitioned into HR. Nola quickly advanced, becoming an HR Specialist and deepening her technical expertise in the field.

Nola sought informal mentors like Cindy, the Training Office supervisor, who encouraged her to apply for a position in the Training Office. It was there that Nola discovered her passion for helping others grow. She thrived in the role, took on stretch assignments, and expanded her network. Over time, Nola became well-known within the agency, and Robyn, the HR Director, encouraged her to participate in the Cleveland Federal Community

Leadership Institute (CFCLI), an intergovernmental, community-based leadership development program for federal employees, where she later served as co-director.

Nola's career continued to evolve with a detail in the Office of STEM Engagement, followed by a role in the Office of Diversity and Equal Opportunity (ODEO). She earned a certification as a Master Game Changer in diversity and inclusion, and upon returning to HR as an

Organization Development Specialist, she was able to apply those valuable skills.

Eventually, Nola applied for and became the Center Learning Officer, a position she has held for four years. With more than 33 years of public service in progressively complex roles, Nola is viewed as a valued contributor and subject matter expert in learning and development across the agency and the greater Cleveland community. She was recently honored with the Influential Leadership Award.

When reflecting on her career journey, Nola emphasized the following key points:

- She proactively sought mentors and advocates who challenged her to exceed her perceived limitations.

- She participated in various learning and development programs that fostered her growth.

- She consistently sought constructive feedback to ensure she was excelling in her current roles and maintaining high performance.

- She received help aligning her career goals with available opportunities within the organization from supervisors, mentors, and coaches, who advocated for her.

- She embraced every opportunity with an open mindset, setting clear career goals and cultivating relationships that contributed to her success.

- Having received support from many throughout her career, she is deeply committed to 'paying it forward' by nurturing and empowering the next generation of leaders.

Lessons from the Trenches

- **Lesson:** Employees notice when leaders invest in their development through mentorship, training, and opportunities for advancement.

- **Impact:** Supporting growth not only improves individual skills but also strengthens the team and organization as a whole.

- **Lesson:** Employees often seek opportunities for growth and development. Leaders can learn from this desire by prioritizing their own and their team's ongoing learning.

- **Impact:** Emphasizing continuous learning keeps skills relevant, encourages personal and professional growth, and enhances overall team capability.

For Reflection:

Regardless of an organization's size, career development is crucial for its ability to evolve, innovate, and thrive. The following questions are designed to help leaders evaluate the effectiveness of their current career development programs:

1. How does leadership influence the promotion of a culture that is focused on continuous learning and career development?

2. In what ways can leaders ensure career development efforts are aligned with the organization's strategic objectives?

3. How can feedback from employees be used to enhance career development programs?

4. How do mentorship and coaching initiatives support sustained career growth?

5. What key metrics should be used to assess the success of a career development program?

6. What potential obstacles could hinder career development efforts, and how can they be addressed?

7. How can organizations cater to the diverse career development needs of their workforce?

CONCLUSION: APPLIED LEADERSHIP

Our mindset influences the beliefs and assumptions we hold about ourselves, others, and the world around us. Without a shift in mindset, change can feel out of reach. What deeply ingrained beliefs are you ready to challenge to accomplish your mission, goals, or purpose?

~ Dr. Marlena N. Hudson, author, coach, and motivational speaker

Leadership lessons hold no real value without action. Understanding these lessons is just the beginning; applying them in your leadership journey and sharing them with your team is crucial. The concept of "leading from the trenches" highlights that true leadership is not developed solely through formal education or high-level strategies but is shaped by working through challenges, making tough decisions, and navigating the complexities of real-world dynamics.

Throughout this book, employees have been placed at the center of leadership. Their experiences, stories, and lessons serve as a guide for leaders looking to improve organizational efficiency and win the trust and loyalty of their teams.

Key takeaways include:

- Winning the hearts and minds of employees requires leaders to understand themselves, especially their core motivations for leading.

- Mastering the ego is essential. Effective leaders avoid the temptation to dominate or seek validation, which develops even stronger leadership skills.

- Building authentic, trust-based relationships is vital for leaders to connect meaningfully with employees and colleagues.

- Leaders must inspire and guide their teams toward shared goals, engage in strategic planning, and lead large-scale change efforts that create value for the organization.

- Effective communication through active listening, empathy, and storytelling is crucial for fostering understanding and connection within teams.

- Leaders who delegate well demonstrate confidence in their teams, promoting a sense of ownership and driving innovation and productivity.

- Putting people first equips employees to achieve organizational goals and objectives, leading to greater engagement, reduced turnover, and improved customer satisfaction.

- Cultivating a culture of career development boosts productivity, succession planning, and competitiveness, ensuring long-term success for the organization.

In conclusion, this book reminds leaders that intentional development—both for themselves and those they lead—is essential in the continuous journey of leadership.

LEADERSHIP LESSONS FROM THE TRENCHES: A FOLLOWER'S PERSPECTIVE

For those who embark on the leadership journey, the following represents a compilation of valuable insights from the perspective of followers. Recognizing these lessons is one step, but putting them into practice is another. I hope that each of you will incorporate these lessons into your leadership development to enhance your effectiveness and efficiency in your role.

Chapter 1: Effective Leadership

Lessons from the Trenches

- **Lesson:** Employees on the frontlines often have a deep understanding of the customer experience, operational inefficiencies, and potential improvements.

- **Impact:** Leveraging this knowledge can help leaders make more informed decisions and improve processes.

- **Lesson:** Effective leaders show understanding and consideration for their team members' feelings and perspectives. They recognize that employees are human beings with unique needs, and they act with compassion.

- **Lesson:** Empathy builds trust and fosters a supportive environment, making employees feel seen, valued, and understood.

Chapter
2: The Humble Leader: Tame Your Ego

Lessons from the Trenches

- **Lesson:** Employees appreciate leaders who are humble, open to feedback, and willing to learn from their team.

- **Impact:** Humility helps leaders build stronger connections, foster a culture of mutual respect, and create a more collaborative environment.

- **Lesson:** Employees respect leaders who "walk the talk." When leaders demonstrate the values and work ethic they expect from their team, it sets a standard for behavior.

- **Impact:** This consistency creates a culture of integrity and motivates employees to mirror those positive behaviors.

Chapter 3: Mastering the Art of Connection

Lessons from the Trenches

- **Lesson:** Sharing personal stories or being open about challenges fosters authenticity. Vulnerability creates a safe space for others to share their experiences, leading to more meaningful connections.

- **Impact:** This deepens trust and paves the way for more genuine relationships, which can inspire creativity, collaboration, and personal growth.

- **Lesson:** Leaders who master connection are better able to inspire, motivate, and influence others.

Chapter

- **Impact:** These behaviors enhance productivity and morale and create a sense of community, leading to high retention rates and increased productivity.

4: Uncharted Territory

Lessons from the Trenches

- **Lesson:** Leaders with a clear vision and strategic mindset inspire employees by providing direction and purpose. They can articulate where the team or organization is headed and why.

- **Impact:** A clear vision motivates employees to align their efforts with the broader goals of the organization.

- **Lesson:** Leaders must be able to adapt quickly, innovate, and empower their teams to experiment and learn.

- **Impact:** When leaders openly acknowledge unknowns while encouraging calculated risk-taking, it creates a culture where employees feel safe to contribute ideas and challenge the status quo without fear of failure.

Chapter 5: Essential Communications: The Key to Success and Collaboration

Lessons from the Trenches

- **Lesson:** Clear, transparent, and consistent communication from leaders is crucial. Employees notice when leaders communicate expectations, provide feedback, and listen actively.

Chapter

- **Impact:** Good communication prevents misunderstandings, aligns team goals, and encourages open dialogue.

- **Lesson:** Employees often highlight the impact of communication, whether it is the need for clarity in expectations or the importance of feedback.

- **Impact:** Leaders can refine their communication skills to ensure alignment, reduce misunderstandings, and foster a more collaborative environment.

6: Distributed Power

Lessons from the Trenches

- **Lesson:** Trusting employees with responsibilities and empowering them to make decisions is a hallmark of strong leadership. Leaders who delegate effectively show confidence in their team's abilities.

- **Impact:** Empowered employees feel more engaged and are likely to take ownership of their work, leading to higher productivity and innovation

- **Lesson:** When employees are given autonomy and trust, they often take greater ownership of their work and contribute more creatively.

- **Impact:** Leaders can learn to delegate more effectively, empowering their teams and fostering a culture of accountability and innovation.

Chapter 7: Decrease Subjectivity and Increase Objectivity

Lessons from the Trenches

Chapter

- **Lesson:** Effective leaders hold themselves and others accountable. They ensure that praise and constructive feedback are delivered fairly, without bias.

- **Impact:** This fairness builds a culture of responsibility and trust, where employees feel that they are treated equitably.

8: Honest and Sincere Appreciation

Lessons from the Trenches

- **Lesson**: Every employee—from the board room to the mail room—values recognition for their hard work and contributions. Leaders and organizations alike can benefit from regularly acknowledging and celebrating employee achievements.

- **Impact**: Regular recognition boosts morale, increases job satisfaction, and motivates employees to continually strive for and maintain higher levels of performance and greater results.

Chapter 9: The Career Architect

Lessons from the Trenches

- **Lesson:** Employees notice when leaders invest in their development through mentorship, training, and opportunities for advancement.

Chapter

- **Impact:** Supporting growth not only improves individual skills but also strengthens the team and organization as a whole.

- **Lesson:** Employees often seek opportunities for growth and development. Leaders can learn from this desire by prioritizing their own and their team's ongoing learning.

- **Impact:** Emphasizing continuous learning keeps skills relevant, encourages personal and professional growth, and enhances overall team capability.

LEADERSHIP LESSONS EVALUATION

The Leadership Lessons Evaluation is designed to encourage reflection on different aspects of leadership—both those you already embody and those you aim to develop. Carefully read each statement, then rate yourself based on how strongly you feel you possess each skill. There are no right or wrong answers. Be realistic and honest about your strengths rather than focusing on what you think you should be doing. The results will help you create an Individual Development Plan.

Read each statement below and use the following scale to rate yourself on each element:

1 = Strongly Disagree

2 = Disagree

3 = Neutral

4 = Agree

5 = Strongly Agree

Effective Leadership

I have clear motivations, goals, and ambitions 1 for stepping into a leadership role.	2	3	4	5
My core values guide my decisions as both a 1 leader and an individual.	2	3	4	5
I can clearly describe my leadership style and 1 understand how others perceive it.	2	3	4	5

I effectively balance management and 1 leadership skills in my position.	2	3	4	5
I cultivate strong motivation and commitment 1 within my team to work together toward future-focused goals.	2	3	4	5

Your Score: _____

The Humble Leader: Taming Your Ego

I demonstrate humility in my daily leadership 1 interactions.	2	3	4	5
I handle feedback or criticism well, even when 1 it challenges my ideas or decisions.	2	3	4	5
I am aware of how my ego may interfere with 1 my leadership.	2	3	4	5
I am open to other's perspectives and show 1 vulnerability with my team.	2	3	4	5
I openly admit my mistakes, readily offer 1 apologies, and seek help whenever needed.	2	3	4	5

Your Score: _____

Mastering the Art of Connection

I actively form connections with others. 1	2	3	4	5
I listen to others' stories, gaining insights about 1 them and myself, which strengthens our relationship.	2	3	4	5
I can recognize when strong relationships and 1 trust have been built, as well as when trust has been diminished.	2	3	4	5

I consistently incorporate the three pillars of trust—credibility, integrity, and leadership—into my daily interactions with my team and colleagues.	1	2	3	4	5
I engage in actions and behaviors that help cultivate trust within my team.	1	2	3	4	5

Your Score: _____

Navigating Uncharted Territory

I understand how the organization's vision aligns with its core values and mission.	1	2	3	4	5
I take action to involve stakeholders in shaping the organization's vision.	1	2	3	4	5
I am aware of internal and external factors influencing the organization and take steps to respond proactively.	1	2	3	4	5
I assess the organization's preparedness for change and address potential risks.	1	2	3	4	5
I foster a culture that encourages experimentation, risk-taking, and innovative thinking.	1	2	3	4	5

Your Score: _____

Essential Communication: The Key to Success and Collaboration

I leverage communication to strengthen relationships, shape culture, and drive engagement.	1	2	3	4	5
Empathy influences my approach to communication.	1	2	3	4	5

I incorporate active listening into my communication practices.	1	2	3	4	5
I create an environment where employees feel comfortable expressing differing opinions and concerns.	1	2	3	4	5
My communication aligns with employees' values, concerns, and lived experiences.	1	2	3	4	5

Your Score: _____

Distributed Power

I consistently seek input from my team, and their ideas are actively considered in decisionmaking processes.	1	2	3	4	5
I create opportunities for team members to showcase their strengths and take the lead on projects.	1	2	3	4	5
I am receptive to different perspectives, even when they challenge my views.	1	2	3	4	5
I empower my team to drive organizational objectives forward.	1	2	3	4	5
I apply the Situational Leadership Model to promote delegation and empowerment.	1	2	3	4	5

Your Score: _____

Decrease Subjectivity and Increase Objectivity

I ensure alignment between individual performance goals and company objectives.	1	2	3	4	5
I implement measures to minimize personal biases in performance appraisals.	1	2	3	4	5
I address underperformance while fostering improvement and accountability.	1	2	3	4	5

I engage employees in their performance development and career progression.	1	2	3	4	5
I ensure performance reviews focus on past achievements and future growth.	1	2	3	4	5

Your Score: _____

Honest and Sincere Appreciation

I understand my employees' preferences for rewards and recognition.	1	2	3	4	5
I ensure that recognition aligns clearly with strategic goals.	1	2	3	4	5
I make sure that recognition ceremonies and rituals hold meaningful value for employees.	1	2	3	4	5
I am familiar with the different methods available within my organization to reward and recognize employees.	1	2	3	4	5
I regularly assess recognition practices to ensure they are effective and positively influence employee behavior.	1	2	3	4	5

Your Score: _____

The Career Architect

I foster a culture of continuous learning and career development.	1	2	3	4	5
I ensure that career development efforts align with strategic objectives.	1	2	3	4	5
I gather employee feedback to improve career development programs within my organization.	1	2	3	4	5
I mentor and coach employees to support long-term career growth.	1	2	3	4	5

| I use key metrics to evaluate the success of career development initiatives. | 1 | 2 | 3 | 4 | 5 |

Your Score: _____

With the evaluation now complete, review each lesson area to identify your strengths and areas for growth. Use the following guidelines to support your progress in your leadership journey.

1-14: This is a developmental area. Create a development plan to enhance these skills or assemble a team of individuals who excel in these areas and leverage their strengths to bridge the gaps.

15-19 This is an area for growth, and with intentional focus and commitment, it has the potential to become a strength. Reflect on the lessons tied to each area and integrate them into your leadership practice.

20-25 This area is your leadership superpower and should remain a guiding force in your decision-making and actions to fulfill your organization's mission, goals, or purpose.

REFERENCES

Abdullah, H. (2009). Significant challenges to the effective management of human resource training and development activities. *Journal of International Social Research, 2*(8).

Abdullah, N., Shonubi, O. A., Hashim, R., & Hamid, N. (2016). Recognition and appreciation and its psychological effect on job satisfaction and performance in a Malaysia IT company: systematic review. *IOSR Journal of Humanities and Social Science, 21*(9), 47-55.

Abidi, S., & Joshi, M. (2015). The VUCA company. Jaico Publishing House.

Abou Elnaga, A., & Imran, A. (2014). The impact of employee empowerment on job satisfaction theoretical study. *American Journal of Research Communication, 2*(1), 13-26.

Aguinis, H., Gottfredson, R. K., & Joo, H. (2012). Delivering effective performance feedback: The strengths-based approach. *Business Horizons, 55*(2), 105-111.

Akafo, V., & Boateng, P. A. (2015). Impact of reward and recognition on job satisfaction and motivation. *European Journal of Business and Management, 7*(24), 112-124.

Alvarez, T. E. (1996). A Plan to Improve Employee Performance in an Employment and Training Organization.

Amalia, N. (2021). Employee Engagement: Does It Matter for Your Company? Tada. https://blog.usetada.com/en/employee-engagementdoes-it-matters-for-your-company

Anderson, B. (2024). The Benefits of Knowledge Management in Business. Bloomfire. https://bloomfire.com/blog/benefits-ofknowledge-management

Andreev, I. (2012). Organizational Learning. Valamis. https://www.valamis.com/hub/organizational-learning

Argyris, C. (1977). Double loop learning in organizations. *Harvard Business Review, 55*(5), 115-125.

Arias, C. (2009). Effectiveness and equity: new challenges for social recognition in higher education. *International Journal of Educational and Pedagogical Sciences, 3*(7), 1486-1493.

Ashkenas, R. & Manvile, B. (2019). You Don't Have to Be CEO to Be a Visionary Leader. *Harvard Business Review.* https://hbr.org/2019/04/you-dont-have-to-be-ceo-to-be-a-visionaryleader

Ates, N., Tarakci, M., Porck, J., Knippenberg, D. & Groenen, P. (2019). Why Visionary Leaders Fail. *Harvard Business Review.* https://hbr.org/2019/02/why-visionary-leadership-fails

Baker, E. L., & Murphy, S. A. (2022). Delegation: A Core Leadership Skill. *Journal of Public Health Management and Practice*, 28(4), 430432.

Bennis, W. (1999). The leadership advantage. *Leader to Leader, 12*(2), 18-23.

Bennis, W. G. (2009). On becoming a leader. Basic Books.
Berraies, S., Chaher, M., & Yahia, K. B. (2014). Employee empowerment and its importance for trust, innovation and organizational performance. *Business Management and Strategy, 5*(2), 82-103.

Best, C. K. (2010). Assessing Leadership Readiness Using Developmental Personality Style: A tool for leadership coaching. *International Journal of Evidence Based Coaching & Mentoring, 8*(1).

Bhattacharyya, S. K. (1972). Strategic Planning: Some Operational Considerations. Economic and Political Weekly, M67-M71.

Bopp, M. A., Bing, D., & Forte-Trammell, S. (2009). Agile career development: Lessons and approaches from IBM. Pearson Education.

Brown, B. (2015). Daring Greatly: How the courage to be vulnerable transforms the way we live, love, parent, and lead. Penguin.

Buchel, S., Hebinck, A., Lavanga, M., & Loorbach, D. (2022). Disrupting the status quo: a sustainability transitions analysis of the fashion system. *Sustainability: Science, Practice and Policy, 18*(1), 231-246.

Burke, T., & Brown, B. (Eds.). (2021). You are your best thing: Vulnerability, shame, resilience, and the Black experience. Random House.

Burrows-McCabe, A. (2014). Stepping stones to leadership. *The Learning Forward Journal, 35*(4), 40-43.

Burton, R. M., Obel, B. & Hakonsson, D. D. (2021). Organizational Design: A Step-by-Step Approach (Fourth edition). Cambridge University Press.

Cable, D. (2018). How humble leadership really works. *Harvard Business Review*, (3)2-5.

Canton, J. (2015). Future Bright: Managing the game-changing trends that will transform your world. Da Capo Press, Incorporated.

Carbery, R., & Cross, C. (2017). Human resource development: A concise introduction. Bloomsbury Publishing.

Carnevale, J. B., Huang, L., Crede, M., Harms, P., & Uhl-Bien, M. (2017). Leading to stimulate employees' ideas: A quantitative review of leader-member exchange, employee voice, creativity, and innovative behavior. *Applied Psychology, 66*(4), 517-552.

Cascella, V. (2002). Effective strategic planning. *Quality Progress, 35*(11), 62-67.

Chaleff, I. (2010). The courageous follower (Vol. 16). ReadHowYouWant. com.

Chancellor, J., & Lyubomirsky, S. (2013). Humble beginnings: Current trends, state perspectives, and hallmarks of humility. *Social and Personality Psychology Compass, 7*(11), 819-833.

Chapman, G. (2011). Dr. Chapman on the 5 Languages of Appreciation in the Workplace. YouTube. https://www.youtube.com/watch?app=desktop&v=JsAzJ4h-RXQ&t=13 Chapman, G., & White, P. (2019). The 5 Languages of Appreciation in the Workplace: Empowering Organizations by Encouraging People. Moody Publishers.

Chermack, T. J. (2011). Scenario planning in organizations: how to create, use, and assess scenarios. Berrett-Koehler Publishers.

Chermack, T. J., Lynham, S. A., & Ruona, W. E. (2001). A review of scenario planning literature. *Futures Research Quarterly, 17*(2), 7-32.

Cherry, K. (2024). Id. Ego and Superego: Freud's Elements of Personality. Very Well Mind.

Clifton, J. (2019). Investigating the Dark Side of Stories of 'Good' Leadership: A Discursive Approach to Leadership Gurus' Storytelling. *International Journal of Business Communication 56*(1), SAGE Publications, pp. 82–99.

Collin, K., Van der Heijden, B., & Lewis, P. (2012). Continuing professional development. *International Journal of Training and Development, 16*(3), 155-163.

Conger, S. (2002). Fostering a career development culture: Reflections on the roles of managers, employees, and supervisors. *Career Development International, 7*(6), 371-375.

Covey, S. M. (2006). The Speed of Trust: The One Thing that Changes Everything.

Daniel, T. A., & Metcalf, G. S. (2005). The fundamentals of employee recognition. *Society of Human Resource Management, 1*(1), 7.

Datalligence AI. (2024). Challenges of Traditional Performance Reviews.

Demġrcġ, M. K., & Erbaġ, A. (2010). Employee empowerment and its effect on organizational performance. *In International Symposium on Sustainable Development, 2*(1).

Dennis, K. S. (2016). Cultivating a growth mindset for effective adaptation in today's dynamic workplace. *International Journal on Lifelong Education and Leadership, 2*(2), 1-11.

Dirks, K. T., & Skarlicki, D. P. (2004). Trust in leaders: Existing research and emerging issues. Trust and distrust in organizations: Dilemmas and approaches, 7, 21-40.

Duchi, L., Lombardi, D., Paas, F., & Loyens, S. M. (2020). How a growth mindset can change the climate: The power of implicit beliefs in influencing people's view and actions. *Journal of Environmental Psychology*, 70, 101461.

Elias, S. (2008). Fifty years of influence in the workplace: The evolution of the French and raven power taxonomy. *Journal of Management History, 14*(3), 267-283.

Fairhurst, G. T. (2007). Discursive leadership: In conversation with leadership psychology. SAGE Publications, Incorporated.

Fiedler, F. (1958). Fiedler's contingency theory. Leader attitudes and group effectiveness.

Fisher, C., Amabile, T. & Pillemer, J. (2021). How to Help (Without Micromanaging). *Harvard Business Review*. https://hbr.org/2021/01/how-to-help-without-micromanaging

Flavia, M. & Enachi-Vasluianu, L. (2016). The importance of elements of active listening in didactic communication: a student's perspective.

In CBU International Conference Proceedings, 4, 332. Central Bohemia University.

Forbes. (2024). NASA Holds Press Conference To Announce Astronauts On The ISS To Return On A SpaceX Flight. https://www.youtube.com/watch?v=92QNhmNWZ9c

Freud, S. (1989). The ego and the id (1923). *TACD Journal, 17*(1), 5-22.

Fung Global Retail & Technology. "Deep Dive: The US Retail Revolution Solution," Page 1.

Gallup, Inc. (2021). The American Upskilling Study Empowering Workers for the Jobs of Tomorrow.

Gambetti, R. C., & Biraghi, S. (2015). The CCO: appointed or organic leader? The rise of conversational leadership. *Corporate Communications: An International Journal, 20*(4), 415-430.

Gazda, S. (2002). The Art of Delegating. Society of Human Resource Management.

Globoforce. (2012). Employee Recognition Survey. Society for Human Resource Management.

Goldsmith, M. (2010). What got you here won't get you there: How successful people become even more successful. Profile books.

Gordon, L. (1952). Personal Factors in Leadership. *Journal of Social Psychology*, 36, 245-248.

Graf, D. (1997). Critical success factors for community-based education. *Mid-American Journal of Business*, 12, 3-4.

Greenan, P. (2016). Personal development plans: insights from a casebased approach. *Journal of Workplace Learning, 28*(5), 322-334.

Griffin, T. (2024). People Quit Bosses, Not Jobs: Why Employees Are Frustrated With Leadership in 2024. https://thomasgriffin.com/peoplequit-bosses/

Grote, R. C. (1996). The complete guide to performance appraisal. Amacom.

Grünig, R., & Kühn, R. (2006). The process of strategic planning, p. 47-74. Springer Berlin Heidelberg.

Guilbrandsen, D. (2011). Green Bay Packers: The Complete Illustrated History – Third Edition. Voyageur Press.

Gurchiek, K. (2022). Workers Across Generations are Dissatisfied with Employee Training. *Society of Human Resource Management*.

Gurchiek, K. (2024). Report: Emerging Professionals Well-Prepared for Workforce. *Society of Human Resource Management*.

Gurchiek, K. (2024). Young Employees Not Getting Career Guidance. *Society of Human Resource Management*.

Guskey, T. R. (2002). Does it make a difference? Evaluating professional development. *Educational Leadership, 59*(6), 45-51.

Hackman, M. Z., & Johnson, C. E. (2013). Leadership: A communication perspective. Waveland press.

Hadijah, H. S. (2023). Implementation of talent management as a strategy for achieving company competitive advantage. *International Journal of Artificial Intelligence Research, 6*(1.1), 1-6.

Halim, N. A. A., & Razak, N. A. (2014). Communication Strategies of Women Leaders in Entrepreneurship. *Procedia Social and Behavioral Sciences*, 118, 21-28.

Hall, D. T., & Moss, J. E. (1998). The new protean career contract: Helping organizations and employees adapt. *Organizational Dynamics, 26*(3), 22-37.

Harrison, K. (2013). Why employee recognition is so important. Cutting Edge PR.

Harting, D. (2010). Employees are your most valuable asset.

Heim, U. (2017). Building a reliable innovation engine. McKinsey & Company.

Heinrich, C. J. (2007). False or fitting recognition? The use of highperformance bonuses in motivating organizational achievements. Journal of Policy Analysis and Management: *The Journal of the Association for Public Policy Analysis and Management, 26*(2), 281304.

Hersey, P., & Blanchard, K. H. (1997). Situational leadership. In Dean's Forum (Vol. 12, No. 2, p. 5).

Ho, N. S., & Nguyen, L. T. M. (2021). Challenges in the implementation of peer-to-peer recognition. In SHS Web of Conferences (Vol. 124, p. 08007). EDP Sciences.

Hollander, E. P. (1992). The essential interdependence of leadership and followership. *Current Directions in Psychological Science, 1*(2), 71-75.

Hoppe, M. H. (2006). Active Listening: Improve Your Ability to Listen and Lead. Greensboro: Center for Creative Leadership.

House, R. J. (1996). Path-goal theory of leadership: Lessons, legacy, and a reformulated theory. *The Leadership Quarterly, 7*(3), 323-352.

Howe, D. (2012). Empathy: What it is and why it matters. Bloomsbury Publishing.

https://www.mckinsey.com/capabilities/operations/ourinsights/building-a-reliable-innovation-engine

Hudson, M. (2024). Practical Tips for Becoming a Full-Range Leader. Regent University.

Hughes, D. J., Lee, A., Tian, A. W., Newman, A., & Legood, A. (2018). Leadership, creativity, and innovation: A critical review and practical recommendations. *The Leadership Quarterly, 29*(5), 549-569.

Implications for performance, teams, and leadership. *Organization Science, 24*(5), 1517-1538.

Incentive Marketing Association. (n.d.). How Top Companies Reward Employees.
https://www.incentivemarketing.org/RPI/Education/Blog_Entries/How_Top_Companies_Reward_Employees.aspx

International Listening Association. (n.d.). Listening Toolkit. https://www.listen.org/listening-toolkit

INTOO. (2023). Unlocking Organizational Success by Supporting Employee Growth and Development.
https://www.intoo.com/us/blog/unlocking-organizational-successreport-press-release/

James, K. T. (2011). Leadership in context: Lessons from new leadership theory and current leadership development practice. King Fund.

Johnston, L. F. (2002). Visionary Leaders. Mc Conkey/Johnson: Inc. Fall.

Jovanovska, S. (2021). Active listening and its implications in the educational process. *Seshadripuram Journal of Social Sciences, 2*(4), 51-60.

Kantabutra, S., & Suriyankietkaew, S. (2012). Examining relationships between organic leadership and corporate sustainability: A proposed model. *Journal of Applied Business Research, 28*(1), 67.

Kanter, R. M. (1992). The challenge of organizational change: How companies experience it, and leaders guide it. Simon and Schuster.

Kaonga, G. (2024). Jeff Bezos called customer service in the middle of a meeting, and the service was uncomfortable. Smart News. https://l.smartnews.com/p-CRgpQ/wJUbmm.

Kavanagh, M. J. (1971). The content issue in performance appraisal: A review. *Personnel Psychology, 24*(4).

Keller, S. and Schaninger, B. (2019). The forgotten step in leading large-scale change. McKinsey & Company.

Kellerman. (2012). The End of Leadership. 1st Edition. HarperCollins Publishers.

Kesebir, P. (2019). Humility: The soil in which happiness grows. Humility, 177-200.

King, A. J. (2010). Follow me! I'm a leader if you do; I'm a failed initiator if you don't. *Behavioral Processes, 84*(3), 671-674.

Klauss, C. P. (2006). Capital investment decisions with managerial overconfidence and regret aversion (Doctoral dissertation, University of Bath).

Kouzes, J. and Posner, B. (1990). The Credibility Factor: What Followers Expect from Their Leaders. Management Review, 79(1).

Kouzes, J. M., & Posner, B. Z. (2006). The leadership challenge (Vol. 3). John Wiley & Sons.

Kouzes, J. M., & Posner, B. Z. (2017). The leadership challenge (Vol. 6). John Wiley & Sons.

Krypa, M. (2017). The Importance of communication cooperation of the leader in the process of leadership in education. *European Journal of Multidisciplinary Studies, 2*(1), 7-14.

Kurtuy, A. (2024). 60+ Career Change Statistics for 2024. Novoresume.com.

Lashway, L. (1997). Leading with Vision. ERIC Clearinghouse on Educational Management.

Lawrence, K. (2013). Developing leaders in a VUCA environment. UNC Executive Development, 1-15.

Lawrence, R. L., & Paige, D. S. (2016). What our ancestors knew: Teaching and learning through storytelling. New Directions for Adult and Continuing Education, 149, 63-72.

Lencioni, P. M. (2010). The five dysfunctions of a team: A leadership fable. John Wiley & Sons.

Lent, R. W., & Brown, S. D. (2013). Understanding and facilitating career development in the 21st century. Career development and counseling: Putting theory and research to work, 2, 1-26.

Lewis, N., Benjamin, W. K., Juda, N., & Marcella, M. (2008). Universities as learning organizations: Implications and challenges. Educational Research and Review, 3(9), 289-293.

Llopis, G. (2017). The innovation mentality: six strategies to disrupt the status quo and reinvent the way we work. Entrepreneur Press.

Llyod, S. (n.d.). Managers Must Delegate Effectively to Develop Employees. *Society of Human Resource Management.*

Louis, K. (2023). Famous Oral Storytellers (Greatest Storytellers of All Time). Branding Design Pro. https://www.brandingdesignpro.com/oralstorytelling

Lunenburg, F. C. (2012). Performance appraisal: Methods and rating errors. *International Journal of Scholarly Academic Intellectual Diversity, 14*(1), 1-9.

Luo, Y., Zhang, Z., Chen, Q., Zhang, K., Wang, Y., & Peng, J. (2022). Humble leadership and its outcomes: A meta-analysis. *Frontiers in Psychology*, 13, 980322.

Mansaray, H. E. (2019). The role of leadership style in organizational change management: a literature review. *Journal of Human Resource Management, 7*(1), 18-31.

Maslyn, J. M., Schyns, B., & Farmer, S. M. (2017). Attachment style and leader-member exchange: the role of effort to build high quality relationships. *Leadership & Organization Development Journal, 38*(3), 450-462.

Masri, N. E., & Abubakr, S. U. L. I. M. A. N. (2019). Talent management, employee recognition and performance in the research institutions. *Studies in Business & Economics, 14*(1).

Maxwell, J. C. (2007). The 21 irrefutable laws of leadership: Follow them and people will follow you. HarperCollins Leadership.

Mayer, R. C., Davis, J. H., & Schoorman, F. D. (1995). An integrative model of organizational trust. *Academy of Management Review, 20*(3), 709-734.

Mayfield, J., Mayfield, M., & Sharbrough, W. C. (2015). Strategic Vision and Values in Top Leaders' Communications: Motivating Language at a Higher Level. *International Journal of Business Communication, 52*(1), 97–121.

McCracken, M., & Wallace, M. (2000). Towards a redefinition of strategic HRD. *Journal of European Industrial Training, 24*(5), 281290.

McLean & Company Insights. (n.d.). Modernize Performance Management.

Merchant Jr, R. C. (2010). The role of career development in improving organizational effectiveness and employee development. *Florida Department of Law Enforcement, 1*(2), 1-17.

Mile, M. (2024). Your guide to what storytelling is and how to be a good storyteller. BetterUp.

Mintzberg, H. (1975). The Manager's Job-folklore and foot. *Harvard Business Review*.

Mitra, A., Gaur, S. S., & Giacosa, E. (2019). Combining organizational change management and organizational ambidexterity using data transformation. *Management Decision, 57*(8), 2069-2091.

Mohapatra, I., & Sundaray, B. K. (2018, March). Impact of employee empowerment on employee performance. In International Journal of Advanced Technology and Engineering Research, National Conference on Recent Trends in Science, Technology and Management, 1, pp. 98102.

Moore, J. R., Maxey, E. C., Waite, A. M., & Wendover, J. D. (2020). Inclusive organizations: developmental reciprocity through authentic leader-employee relationships. *Journal of Management Development, 39*(9/10), 1029-1039.

Morgan, D. (2018). Top 10 Drivers of Innovation. New & Improved Blog Post. Available at: https://newandimproved.com/2018/10/05/top-10-drivers-innovation/

N'Cho, J. (2017). Contribution of talent analytics in change management within project management organizations: The case of the French aerospace sector. *Procedia Computer Science*, 121, 625-629.

Northouse, P. (2022). Leadership Theory and Practice. Thousand Oaks, CA: Sage.

Obisi, C. (2011). Employee performance appraisal and its implication for individual and organizational growth. *Australian Journal of Business and Management Research, 1*(9), 92.

O'Sullivan, D., & Dooley, L. (2008). Applying innovation. Sage publications.

Owens, B. P., Johnson, M. D., & Mitchell, T. R. (2013). Expressed humility in organizations:

Parry, W. (2015). Big change, best path: Successfully managing organizational change with wisdom, analytics and insight. Kogan Page Publishers.

Patricia, O. (2015). Improving interpersonal relationship in workplaces. *Journal of Research & Method in Education, 5*(6), 115-125.

Phillips, J. M., Dlugos, K. E., & Park, H. M. (2023). Recognizing employees. Principles of Organizational Behavior: The Handbook of Evidence-Based Management, 255, 255-270.

Plakhotnik, M. (2014). Organizational culture and HRD. Handbook of Human Resource

Development, 80-93.

Power, C., & Lapsley, D. (1988). Self, ego, and identity. Integrative Approaches. New York.

Price Waterhouse Coopers. (2011). Millennials at work Reshaping the workplace.
https://www.pwc.com/m1/en/services/consulting/documents/millennials-at-work.pdf

Price Waterhouse Coopers. (2022). PwC's Global Workforce Hopes and Fears Survey 2022.
https://www.pwc.com/gx/en/issues/workforce/hopes-and-fears-2022.html

Rabbi, F., Ahad, N., Kousar, T., & Ali, T. (2015). Talent management as a source of competitive advantage. *Journal of Asian Business Strategy, 5*(9), 208-214.

Rahasya, M. K. (2017). Teaching good character in a narrative text through storytelling. *Journal of English and Education, 5*(2), 145-153.

Ramya, S. & Vanithamani, M. (2023). The Power of Employee Recognition: Building A Culture of Appreciation in the Workplace. *Journal of Technical Education*, 109, 109.

Rego, L., & Garau, R. (2007). Stepping into the void. Center for Creative Leadership, 69, 1-76.

Reichheld, F. F. (2001). Loyalty rules!: how today's leaders build lasting relationships. Harvard Business Press.

Reina, D. S. (2009). Trust and betrayal in the workplace: Building effective relationships in your organization. ReadHowYouWant.com.

Richardson, V. (2020). Strategic Foresight: Part 2, Introduction to STEEPLE Analysis (Video). Regent University, School of Business and Leadership.

Riggio, R. E., Chaleff, I., & Lipman-Blumen, J. (2008). The art of followership: How great followers create great leaders and organizations. John Wiley & Sons.

Riisgaard H, Søndergaard J, Munch M, Le JV, Ledderer L, Pedersen LB, Nexøe J. (2017). Work motivation, task delegation and job satisfaction of general practice staff: a cross-sectional study. *Family Practice, 34*(2), p. 188-193.

Robbins, M. (2019). Why employees need both recognition and appreciation. *Harvard Business Review*, 1-5.

Rockwood, K. (2022). How Learning and Development Can Attract—and Retain—Talent. *Society of Human Resource Management*.

Rogers, C. R., & Farson, R. E. (1957). Active listening (p. 84). Chicago, IL: Industrial Relations Center of the University of Chicago.

Rost, J. (1993). Leadership for the twenty-first century. Bloomsbury Publishing USA.

Rost, M., & Wilson, J. J. (2013). Active listening. Routledge.

Rowley, D. J., & Sherman, H. (2002). Implementing the strategic plan. *Planning for Higher Education, 30*(4), 5-14.

Sánchez-Cardona, I., Salanova Soria, M., & Llorens-Gumbau, S. (2018). Leadership intellectual stimulation and team learning: The mediating role of team positive affect. Universitas *Psychologica, 17*(1), 221-236.

Saunderson, R. (2016). Employee recognition: Perspectives from the field.

Schein, E. H., & Schein, P. A. (2018). Humble leadership: The power of relationships, openness, and trust. Berrett-Koehler Publishers.

Schuler, A. J. (2003). Overcoming resistance to change: Top ten reasons for change resistance.

Senge, P. M. (2014). The fifth discipline field book: Strategies and tools for building a learning organization. Crown Currency.

Sivers, D. (2010). First Follower: Leadership Lessons from Dancing Guy. YouTube. https://www.youtube.com/watch?v=fW8amMCVAJQ

Slaughter, R. A. (1997). Developing and applying strategic foresight. ABN Report, 5(10), 13-27.

Snaith, C. (2020). Taming Your Ego. LinkedIn. https://www.linkedin.com/pulse/taming-your-ego-cam-snaith

Sosik, J. J., & Jung, D. (2011). Full range leadership development: Pathways for people, profit and planet. Psychology Press.

Sowcik, M., Carter, H., & McKee, V. (2018). Reframing Recognition in Organizations: AEC662/WC325, 12/2018. EDIS, 2018(6).

Steiner, G. A. (2010). Strategic planning. Simon and Schuster.

Sullivan, J. (1988). Three roles of language in motivation theory. Academy of Management Review, 13, 104–115.

Sulosaari, V., Kosklin, R., & De Munter, J. (2023, February). Nursing leaders as visionaries and enablers of action. In Seminars in Oncology Nursing (Vol. 39, No. 1, p. 151365). WB Saunders.

Syafril, S., & Yaumas, N. E. (2017). Six ways to develop empathy of educators. *Journal of Engineering and Applied Sciences, 12*(7), 16871691.

Tjosvold, D., & Wong, A. S. (2000). The leader relationship: building teamwork with and among employees. *Leadership & Organization Development Journal, 21*(7), 350-354.

Tzouramani, E. (2017). Leadership and empathy. Leadership today: Practices for Personal and Professional Performance, 197-216.

Vaillant, G. E. (1998). The wisdom of the ego. Harvard University Press.

Van der Heijden, K. (2005). Scenarios: the art of strategic conversation. John Wiley & Sons.

Van Velsor, E., McCauley, C. D., & Ruderman, M. N. (Eds.). (2010). The Center for Creative Leadership Handbook of Leadership Development (Vol. 122). John Wiley & Sons.

Van Woerkom M. & Kroon, B. (2020). The Effect of Strengths-Based Performance Appraisal on Perceived Supervisor Support and the Motivation to Improve Performance. Front Psychology 11, 1883.

Venus, M., Stam, D., & Van Knippenberg, D. (2013). Leader emotion as a catalyst of effective leader communication of visions, value-laden messages, and goals. *Organizational Behavior and Human Decision Processes, 122*(1), 53-68.

Vorwig, K. S., & Weichsel, F. (2016). Humble Leadership. Contemporary Practice and Theory of Organizations–Part 2: Leading and Changing the Organization, 39.

Walsh, R. N., & Vaughan, F. (1980). Beyond the ego. *Journal of Humanistic Psychology*, 20.

Walters, K. N., & Diab, D. L. (2016). Humble leadership: Implications for psychological safety and follower engagement. *Journal of Leadership Studies, 10*(2), 7-18.

Walz, G. R. (1982). Career Development in Organizations.

Wang, S., & Luan, K. (2024). How do employees build and maintain relationships with leaders? Development and validation of the workplace upward networking scale. *Journal of Vocational Behavior*, 150, 103985.

Wang, Y., Liu, J., & Zhu, Y. (2018). Humble leadership, psychological safety, knowledge sharing, and follower creativity: a cross-level investigation. *Frontiers in Psychology*, 9, 1727.

Welch, J. (n.d.). AZQuotes.com. Retrieved September 11, 2024, from https://www.azquotes.com/citation/quote/520701

Welch, J. F., Bossidy, L., Weiss, W. & Stratford, M. (1993). The New Era A Master Class in Radical Change Only a few CEOs Have Attempted Corporate Revolution. CNN Money. https://money.cnn.com/magazines/fortune/fortune_archive/1993/12/13/78736/index.htm

White, P. (2016). Appreciation at Work training and the Motivating by Appreciation Inventory: development and validity. *Strategic HR Review, 15*(1), 20-24.

Wickramaratne, W. R. (2013). Role of career development culture and senior management support in career development. *International Journal of Arts and Commerce, 2*(6), 79-84.

Wigert, B. & Dvorak, N. (2019). Feedback is Not Enough. https://www.gallup.com/workplace/257582/feedback-not-enough.aspx

Wikaningrum, T., & Yuniawan, A. (2018). The relationships among leadership styles, communication skills, and employee satisfaction: A study on equal employment opportunity in leadership. *Journal of Business and Retail Management Research, 13*(1), 138-147.

Winston, B. & Patterson, K. (2006). An integrative definition of leadership. *International Journal of Leadership, 1*(2), 6-66.

Wright, J. C. (2019). Humility as a foundational virtue. Humility, 146174.

Zaleznik, A. (2004). Managers and leaders. Harvard Business Review, 1.

Zhang X, Qian J, Wang B, Jin Z, Wang J, Wang Y. (2017). Leaders' Behaviors Matter: The Role of Delegation in Promoting Employees' Feedback-Seeking Behavior. *Front Psychology, 8*(920).

ABOUT THE AUTHOR

Dr. Marlena N. Hudson is an accomplished strategist in leadership development, with a focus on empowering individuals, teams, and organizations. She is the author of *Leadership Lessons from the Trenches: A Follower's Perspective*, a guide designed to help leaders at all levels enhance their leadership capacity.

As a strategy consultant, executive coach, and motivational speaker, Dr. Hudson specializes in human behavior dynamics, with a strong emphasis on leadership development, coaching, and driving change across personal, team, and organizational levels.

In her role at NASA's John H. Glenn Research Center, she leads the Talent Services organization, where she plays a critical role in shaping leadership and talent strategies. Dr. Hudson is also the founder and CEO of Elevate You Training and Consulting Services, LLC, a firm dedicated to developing high-performance leaders.

With a diverse background spanning government, banking, and nonprofit sectors, she brings expertise in human capital strategy, learning and development, organizational development, change management, performance management, employee and labor relations, and employee engagement.